PUT ON CHRIST

PUT ON CHRIST

LIFE AS DISCIPLESHIP

Antonio Pitta

Paulist Press
New York / Mahwah, NJ

Cover design by Tamian Wood
Book design by Lynn Else

Library of Congress Cataloging-in-Publication Data
Names: Pitta, António, author.
Title: Put on Christ : life as discipleship / António Pitta.
Other titles: Rivestirsi di Cristo. English
Description: New York : Paulist Press, 2020. | Includes bibliographical references. | Summary: "Put on Christ encourages us to be one in Christ and removes the boundaries between Jew and Greek, slave and free, and even sexual barriers between male and female"— Provided by publisher.
Identifiers: LCCN 2019022451 (print) | LCCN 2019022452 (ebook) | ISBN 9780809154791 (paperback) | ISBN 9781587688911 (ebook)
Subjects: LCSH: Jesus Christ—Example—Meditations. | Christian life—Catholic authors—Meditations.
Classification: LCC BT304.2 .P5813 2020 (print) | LCC BT304.2 (ebook) | DDC 248.4—dc23
LC record available at https://lccn.loc.gov/2019022451
LC ebook record available at https://lccn.loc.gov/2019022452

ISBN 978-0-8091-5479-1 (paperback)
ISBN 978-58768-891-1 (e-book)

Published by Paulist Press
997 Macarthur Boulevard
Mahwah, New Jersey 07430
www.paulistpress.com

Printed and bound in the
United States of America

I wanted to read no further, nor did I need to. For instantly, as the sentence ended, there was infused in my heart something like the light of full certainty and all the gloom of doubt vanished away.

St. Augustine, *Confessions* 8, 12, 29

Contents

Foreword ix
Beniamino Cardinal Stella

Preface xi

1. The Humanity of Jesus Christ in the Life of the Apostle 1

2. Conformed to His Glorious Body 14

3. The Paschal Mystery in the Life of the Apostle 24

4. The Paradox of Grace 35

5. Manifestations of the Spirit 49

6. Our Thirst Has Been Quenched with One Spirit 61

Conclusion 79

Notes 85

Bibliography 89

Foreword

The word *disciple* occurs about three hundred times in the four Gospels. It denotes, in fact, the response to a call by Jesus to share in the Father's plan that he came to accomplish. Moreover, it defines the traits of that group of people who, leaving everything behind, welcomed his invitation and followed him. Therefore, this evangelical term is not simply one among many, but of itself can synthesize a characteristic element of the faith: to believe means to walk behind the Lord, sharing in the experience of God's love revealed in Jesus, thereby allowing our entire being to be touched and molded. It is for this reason that, by welcoming the Magisterium of Pope Francis in the *Ratio Fundamentalis*, promulgated two years ago by the Congregation for the Clergy, priestly formation is considered anew in terms of discipleship.

This essential priestly feature must shine forth in the personal life of piety of each priest and in the specific mission entrusted to him, irrespective of the conditions, the location, and the ecclesial reality of his ministry. With this in mind, I consider it opportune that those priests who are called to serve the Church and the Holy Father in the Roman Curia can take advantage of a space for prayer, where they can listen to and meditate on the Word of God, courtesy of three retreats offered by the Secretariat of State and the Congregation for the Clergy.

The following pages are the fruit of the retreat preached this year by Antonio Pitta, tenured professor and scholar of New Testament exegesis at the Pontifical Lateran University. They comprise a series of meditations offered during retreat days held over the past year that focused on the theme of discipleship, as imitation of Christ and conformity to him, evidenced through the life, ministry, and preaching of the Apostle Paul.

In helping us to overcome a reductive and moralistic vision of the imitation of Christ, along with a prejudicial and partial reading of the topic, Professor Pitta expounds the veracity of this theme that emerges as a dominant motif in the Pauline Epistles. To be in Christ by the power of the Holy Spirit, as the author notes, makes the believer an Icon of the Lord. One should not think of imitation simply as a copy of an original—impossible to realize, thus running the risk of reducing Christ to a mere "model"—but as an intimate relationship that engenders an endless process of conformity to Christ in the life of believers.

In this perspective, Paul's apostolic ministry complements the Synoptic interpretation of discipleship, namely, that in following the Lord and being incorporated into him through baptism, one is conformed to him. This present text affords the reader an opportunity to experience, in a singular fashion, what it means to be a believer in Christ. Accepting his invitation to follow him involves a gradual transformation of one's identity through the power of the Holy Spirit, who reaches into the wounds, the weaknesses of the flesh, and the imperfections of our human condition.

In fact, this is the journey of St. Paul, that champion of Christianity. Professor Pitta demonstrates how the apostle of the Gentiles leads us on a sort of pilgrimage from the humanity of Jesus, viewed through the lens of the pascal mystery, to the superabundance of God's grace that places the treasure of the gospel in the fragile earthen vessel of our lives. As this mystery unfolds, the humanity of God and our humanity entwine, with God's grace, as St. Paul says, perfecting our human weakness. The following pages, the fruit of sound biblical exegesis, are filled with intensity and a passion that will warm the heart of the reader.

I avail myself of this opportunity to convey my heartfelt gratitude to Professor Antonio Pitta for the proficiency and the skillfulness with which he conducted our spiritual exercises this year, and for the beauty of this text, which can accompany every minister and priest in the pathway of discipleship and conformity to Christ the Lord.

Beniamino Cardinal Stella

Preface

It gives me great pleasure to publish the following lecture delivered to priests of the Roman Curia during the seasons of Advent, Lent, and Easter. The common thread of the following meditations is the conformity between Jesus Christ, the apostle, and believers as it is expounded in the following three Pauline Epistles: Philippians, 2 Corinthians, and 1 Corinthians. The theme chosen belongs to what was once called "the imitation of Christ," one of the preferred pathways in the past for Christian spirituality. For example, *The Imitation of Christ*, attributed to Thomas à Kempis (fifteenth century), received great prominence in the history of spirituality until the last century.

Sadly, the theme of imitation has fallen into oblivion in recent decades, due to various misunderstandings. Today, we are reluctant to imitate other people because we want above all to be original and we forget that imitation is integral to human nature. Over time, unfortunately, the idea of imitation has gone from that of becoming connatural to being viewed in terms of superiority and morality, as if it depended on the authority of the model to be imitated or the choice of the one who has decided to imitate him. Imitation or mimesis is the result of chosen affinity and conformity among people who grow daily by spending time together. The philosopher Seneca (first century CE), in one of his letters, exhorts Lucilius, his disciple:

> Choose a master whose life, conversation, and soul-expressing face have satisfied you; picture him always to yourself as your protector or your pattern. For we must indeed have someone

> according to whom we may regulate our characters; you can never straighten that which is crooked unless you use a ruler.[1]

Chosen affinity between people is at the root of human and artistic imitation. For this reason, imitation is not the result of a certain morality but the exact opposite: conformity of life produces imitation in understanding, in actions, and in words. Suffice it to consider any artistic product: in order to mature, it requires the technique and the exertion of perfecting the work, but it stems from the assimilation between the material or nature and the artist. Without the inspiration that unites nature and reality to art, no technique could be applied and it would be impossible to produce an authentic imitation.

A further misconception inflicted upon the spirituality of imitation is the fear of compromising one's own uniqueness: "Beware of imitations" is the advertisement for pickles, evoked by Robert Barr in *The Clue of the Silver Spoons*, the novel written at the beginning of the last century (1909). Transferred to human relationships, *beware of imitation* signals the reluctance to imitate another person for fear that one's uniqueness could be diminished and lost. Staying with the artistic product, with all its defects, the so-called contemporary mimetic art contains an undeniable truth: the conjoining of reality and technique makes imitation possible.

Paul of Tarsus made the imitation of Christ one of the main themes in his letters: being in Christ, through the Holy Spirit, makes the believer and the apostle another Christ (*alter Christus*) or an icon of Christ. While the Gospels outline the relationship between Jesus of Nazareth and his disciples in terms of following and discipleship, where one follows another, Paul chooses the paradigm of imitation between Christ, the believer, and the apostle to express the same condition. Even if he did not have the opportunity to meet Jesus of Nazareth in person, Paul chooses the pattern of conformity to convey the same relationship with the risen Christ. The idea of following and conformity are correlated because they share the same footprints, the same itinerary, and the same goal. As Dietrich Bonhoeffer correctly observed,

> The Jesus of the Synoptics is neither nearer nor further from us than the Christ of St Paul. The Christ who is present is the Christ of the whole Scripture. He is the incarnate, crucified, risen, and glorified Christ, and he meets us in his word. The difference between the terminology of the Synoptics and the witness of St Paul does not involve any break in the unity of Scriptural testimony. Where the Synoptic Gospels speak of Christ calling men and their following him, St Paul speaks of Baptism.[2]

We see the dichotomy between an awareness of the imitation of Christ and the contrary response among his first disciples. They followed him during his public ministry but betrayed him and fled when they were faced with the cross of Jesus Christ. When someone gives up his discipleship, he needs to go to Galilee where the risen One preceded his disciples and called them anew to follow him. In fact, the first announcement about the risen Christ is, "He is going ahead of you into Galilee. There you will see him, just as he told you" (Mark 16:7). Similarly, according to the Gospel of John, Peter was asked to follow Jesus not at the beginning of his public life, as for the other Gospels (cf. Mark 1:16—18; Matt 4:18—20; Luke 5:10—11), but after his resurrection: "Follow me!" (John 21:19, 22).

Without doubt, as Ernst Käsemann (1965) held, Christ is the archetype and not the model. However, this kind of view has caused the rash abandonment of the idea of imitation or of mimesis. Christ is inimitable precisely because he is the archetype, and it is intimacy with him that engenders in the believer, and the apostle, an endless process of imitation. When one is liberated from the blind alleyways of authority, morality, and devaluation, human imitation understood as discipleship has much to impart to Christian spirituality. As a precondition for this, imitation must pertain, from the outset, to the realm of intimacy, to regular encounter, and to the uniqueness of each person before the archetype.

"Be imitators of me as I am of Christ" (1 Cor 11:1), exhorted Paul, who begot many people in faith through his gospel of Christ (see 1 Thess 3:2). An affirmation like that is only possible where there is intimacy between persons, without which there would ensue the hesitancy of not being capable of imitating Jesus Christ perfectly. Yet it is these same imperfections that highlight the uniqueness of the one who follows the model.

To better convey the idea of intimacy, as a condition for imitation, Paul uses the metaphor of giving birth, as this unites him to the community that he has generated by faith in Christ (see 1 Thess 2:7—11; 1 Cor 4:15—17; 2 Cor 6:13; Gal 4:19). He does not see himself as a mere pedagogue or teacher (see 1 Cor 4:15), with all due respect for the role that this has in human formation, but as a father who admonishes or as a mother who gives birth to faith.

The beauty of discipleship is captured in this new understanding of imitation in terms of conformity to Christ. Conformity is neither a vacuous beauty that mimics the original, nor one of empty perfection, but rather a beauty that undergoes various trials and injuries. As these are healed with the passage of time, we come to recognize those who are true imitators. The following chapters are dedicated to this understanding of imitation as conformity: from the assimilation between Christ and our humanity, to our assimilation of his humility and obedience; from the sharing of his weakness on the cross to participation in his resurrection; and from the creative action of the Holy Spirit to charisms, ministries, and activities generated by his power in the Church (see 1 Cor 12:11). Without the Holy Spirit, the body formed by believers risks remaining dehydrated and inanimate.

The title of the following meditations evokes one of the most insightful metaphors about the imitation of Christ, used twice by Paul in his epistles. Those who are baptized are clothed in Christ (see Gal 3:27), and for this reason, they are called to continue to put on Jesus Christ daily (see Rom 13:14). The metaphor is original and audacious because it refers not to a theatrical context, wherein one is clothed in the garments of the person being represented, but rather to the intimacy that exists between the risen Lord and believers. Expressed differently, in Christ, the old man is removed to give way to the new man (see Col 3:10; Eph 4:24). At first glance, this metaphor might appear to lend a superficial understanding to conformity between Christ and believers. To clothe oneself in Christ could appear to refer solely to external and visible appearances as opposed to the interiority of the human being. We are speaking here of a visibility that originates from the newness of being one with Christ, overcoming ethnic and juridical barriers between Jew and Greek, social barriers between slave and free, and even sexual barriers between male and female (see Gal 3:27). Be what you are! It is the essential meaning of clothing with Christ.

The change in one's identity implies a transformation of one's modus operandi. Because one is already clothed in Christ through baptism, one is encouraged to continue being clothed in Christ, to the point of being clothed in the entrails of mercy (see Col 3:12) and with the armor of justice (see Eph 6:14). Understood thus, the metaphor conveys one of the most original characteristics of conformity and imitation between Christ and believers. While our outer human condition may be falling into decay, our inner human nature is, at the same time, renewed day by day (see 2 Cor 4:16–17). The metaphor of putting on Christ has been so enlightening that St. Augustine of Hippo passionately seized upon it at the climax of his conversion, as we read in his *Confessions*:

> So I quickly returned to the bench where Alypius was sitting, for there I had put down the apostle's book when I had left there. I snatched it up, opened it, and in silence read the paragraph on which my eyes first fell: *Not in rioting and drunkenness, not in chambering and wantonness, not in strife and envying, but put on the Lord Jesus Christ, and make no provision for the flesh to fulfill the lusts thereof.* I wanted to read no further, nor did I need to. For instantly, as the sentence ended, there was infused in my heart something like the light of full certainty and all the gloom of doubt vanished away.[3]

I am heartily grateful to His Eminence, Beniamino Cardinal Stella, and to those who exercise their service in the Secretariat of State and in the Congregation for the Clergy, who afforded me the opportunity to share with priests of the Roman Curia these meditations on imitation understood as following Christ. A certain dread about the first meditation soon gave way to a fruitful exchange on St. Paul's thought, who for many is the

Christian genius and the incomparable imitator of Christ. My gratitude also goes to the superiors and seminarians at the Pontifical Urban College *de Propaganda Fide* in Rome, with whom I have also shared some of these meditations. My intense desire is that, despite our difficulties, weaknesses, and poverty, every believer and priest in our time will rediscover the beauty of imitating Christ, growing daily in intimacy with him.

1

The Humanity of Jesus Christ in the Life of the Apostle

Imagine standing at the entrance of the gorgeous Basilica of St. Paul outside the Walls in Rome and looking at the majestic mosaic of the apse. St. Paul indicates the Lord Jesus Christ to the visitor while holding a parchment. The parchment contains the following inscription: *In nomine Iesu omne genu flectatur caelestium, terrestrium et infernorum* (At the name of Jesus every knee should bow, in heaven and on earth and under the earth). The phrase belongs to the second part of the oldest song or hymn devoted to the Lord Jesus Christ in the Church, namely, Philippians 2:5–11.

The believers of the first Christian generation gave worship to Christ with the bending of their knees and the confession of their faith in him. Our attention is particularly attracted by the first part of the eulogy (rather than hymn) of Christ Jesus. According to a more careful version of the Greek text, the eulogy sings as follows:

> Have in you the same mindset as [it] is in Christ Jesus, who, being in the form of God, did not consider being equal to God a thing to be grasped, but he emptied himself having assumed the form of a slave, having become in assimilation with men;

and being found in appearance as a man, he humbled himself by becoming obedient until death, even death on a cross!

Therefore, God exalted him to the highest place and gave him the name that is above every name, that at the name of Jesus every knee should bow in heaven and on earth and under the earth, and every tongue confess: Jesus Christ the Lord, to the glory of God the Father. (Phil 2:5–11)

What of Christ Jesus is poured out into our humanity? And what can conform us to him, so as to create an unending process of imitation that lasts throughout our life? Contemplating the humanity of Christ is to glimpse the condition and conformity of our humanity to him.

WHAT OF CHRIST'S HUMANITY?

Usually, Paul does not pay too much attention to the incarnation, birth, and human traits of Jesus of Nazareth. Concentrated as he is on the death and resurrection of Christ, he focuses on "the word of the cross" (see 1 Cor 1:18) or on the urgency to preach Christ, and him crucified (see 1 Cor 1:23). In passing, he remembers the Son of God was born of a woman and under the Mosaic Law to redeem those who were under the Law, so that they may receive his Sonship (see Gal 4:4–6). According to one of the so-called sending formulas used by Paul, God sent his Son in the assimilation of sinful flesh and thus he condemned sin in the flesh (see Rom 8:3). In a process of a paradoxical interchange between Christ and believers, Paul highlights the grace of Christ. Though he was rich, yet for our sake he became poor, so that through his poverty we might become rich (see 2 Cor 8:9). Such an interchange is humanly inconceivable because we have never seen a poor man capable of enriching other people.

The mystery of incarnation again echoes at the end of the Letter to the Romans when, in exhorting the strong and the weak of Christian communities to welcome each other, Paul emphasizes how they were welcomed by Christ (see Rom 15:7). In fact, Jesus made himself a servant of circumcision and of the Jewish people to show God's faithfulness and to confirm the promises made to their fathers. Consequentially, Gentiles may glorify God for his mercy or election (see Rom 15:8–9). We ought not to think as if Paul was not interested in the humanity of Jesus Christ. Rather, he prefers to rethink the life of Christ from the end and not from the beginning, because the identity of Christ's humanity is revealed from the end more than from the beginning.

Divinity becoming human has always been incomprehensible to ancient and new religions. We can remember the ironic perspective of Plautus's *Amphitryon* (third century BCE). In that comedy, Jupiter appears in the guise of Amphitryon, and Mercury in that of his servant to deceive Amphitryon and his wife. However, when they feel in danger, they reveal to Amphitryon who they are: gods and not human beings. A simple appearance dressed as a servant showed their empty humanity (Plautus, *Amphitryon*, 117). The contrast between Plautus's comedy about the divine appearing in the form of a servant and the human condition to which Jesus Christ assimilated himself is radical. Christ Jesus's humanity is not an apparent form of a human being, as it is for Gnosticism, but it is an integral form or the condition of slavery: from the beginning to the end of his earthly life.

Unfortunately, the Greek noun *homoiōma* used in Philippians 2:7 is rendered misleadingly as "likeness" or "similar" as if the humanity assumed by Christ should be understood as a kind of resemblance or appearance and not reality. On the contrary, the so-called eulogy of Christ of Philippians 2:6–11 intends to assert quite the opposite. The humanity of Christ was not similar to our condition, but it was a full assimilation into our humanity. If he had not assimilated himself into our humanity, in all things but sin, he could not have defeated sin in the flesh (see Rom 8:3).

At first glance, because all human beings are sinners, Jesus's humanity seems partial and not complete. How could a person be considered a man if he did not know sin like all human beings (see 2 Cor 5:21; Heb 4:15)? However, sin does not bring about any communion between people, not even the sin committed between two or more individuals. On the contrary, sin always creates a personal and relational division, and we recognize sin not from statutes, nor by a list of commandments, but by the effects of the division it produces. This is the everlasting message given by the first pages of Scripture. Sin always produces a split between Adam and Eve, human beings and nature, creatures and Creator (see Gen 3:14–19; Rom 1:18–32). Therefore, precisely because he did not sin, Christ Jesus realized a full communion and a deep assimilation with human beings.

Using sacerdotal categories, the author of the Letter to the Hebrews deepens Christ's humanity in the following way. To become a merciful and faithful high priest, Jesus was not "made like" (as, e.g., in the NIV, NJB, and NIRV), but he "assimilated" himself to the brethren in all things but sin (see Heb 2:17). It is not by chance that the verb used in Hebrews 2:17 is related to the noun chosen by Paul in Romans 8:3 and Philippians 2:7. Assimilation rather than similarity is the result of the relationship between Christ and our humanity. Once again, the process of assimilation between Christ and humanity is underscored. This kind of assimilation reached its peak when Jesus Christ, though he was a Son, learned obedience from what he suffered (see Heb 5:8). Christ assimilated himself to his brethren through his obedience, and, made perfect, he became a cause of salvation for all those who obey him (see Heb 5:9).

Christ's sacrifice does not consist in a privation of something, but in a transformation of what is profane into something sacred and holy. This is the reason why his sacrifice is the starting point of his priesthood and not the opposite. He was not first a priest who afterward sacrificed himself for our sins, but because he sacrificed himself in unconditional obedience, he became the one and only high and eternal priest, according to the brilliant intuition of the author of the Epistle to the Hebrews. In fact, Jesus descended from the tribe of Judah, and no one from that tribe could serve at the altar except those from the tribe of Levi (see Heb 7:13–14). At any rate, the perfecting of Christ is not regarding his divine nature, but his sacrifice, because it alludes to the conditions required of the victims for sacrifice in the Old Testament: "They must not have any flaws" or defects (Lev 9:2; Num 6:14).

Therefore, this kind of perfection is the climax of Jesus's assimilation to our humanity and not the beginning. He "became perfect" through his conformity to our humanity. Christ assimilated himself to a full and perfect humanity: an assimilation that starts from his divine condition (more than nature), it passes through his human condition and ends with death on a cross. The mystery of the incarnation is never conceived as disjointed or separated from the paschal mystery. On the contrary, it is always directed toward the death and resurrection of Christ. Because he was born from the seed of David, Jesus Christ was constituted Son of God by the resurrection of the dead (see Rom 1:3–4).

The traits of our humanity have been assimilated by Jesus Christ to the point of his manifestation of God's benevolence and love for humanity, as the other hymn of the ancient Church reminds us: "But when the benevolence and philanthropy of God our Savior appeared, he saved us not by virtue of works of justice, accomplished by us, but because of his mercy" (Titus 3:4–5).

A COURSE OF DISHONOR

The course of honor dominated the urban and civic life in the imperial period. The career for a course of honor could only be accomplished by the members of high classes of Roman society, like nobles, senators, and equites. On the contrary, a course of honor was forbidden to the lower classes of slaves, freedmen, and workers. Paradoxically, the eulogy of Christ exalts his course of ignominy and dishonor: a *course of ignominy* instead of a *course of honor*. In fact, Jesus Christ passes from the divine condition and divine form to the form of a slave, namely, from the highest level of his divine status to the lowest level of the social classes.

The song for Christ seems to have been recorded with fidelity in Philippians 2:6–11, as it was handed down to Paul by one of the first Christian communities. Scholars have proposed the communities of Jerusalem or Antioch of Syria. However, according to most commentators, a decisive correction has been added that even more underscores Christ's course of dishonor: "even death on a cross" (v. 8c). In fact, the correction seems a gloss or an insertion, added by Paul, which interrupts the sequence of the verbs and specifies the kind of death suffered by Christ. As if to say he could not get below that lowest status, and he assimilated himself not only to our humanity, but also to slaves. We ought to remember in the ancient world slaves were considered not as human beings, but as objects and instruments in the hands of their masters. In his *Politics*, Aristotle (fourth century BCE) explains the idea of "natural slavery" in Greek society as follows:

> The intention of nature therefore is to make the bodies also of freemen and of slaves different—the latter strong for necessary service, the former erect and unserviceable for such occupations, but serviceable for a life of citizenship (and that again divides into the employments of war and those of peace); though as a matter of fact often the very opposite comes about. Slaves have the bodies of freemen and freemen the souls only; since this is certainly clear, that if freemen were born as distinguished in body as are the statues of the gods, everyone would say that those who were inferior deserved to be these men's slaves.[1]

Moreover, crucifixion was the capital punishment reserved for traitors, criminals, and slaves and it was known as a slave's punishment. In his defense of the senator Gaius Rabirius, Cicero (first century BCE) recommends,

> Even if death is set before us, we may die free men. But the executioner, the veiling of heads, and the very word "cross" should be far removed from not only the bodies of Roman citizens but even from their thoughts, their eyes, and their ears. The results and suffering from these doings as well as the situation, even anticipation, of their enablement, and, in the end, the mere mention of them are unworthy of a Roman citizen and a free man.[2]

On the contrary, Sceledrus the slave of Plautus's *The Braggart Warrior* confesses, "Enough of your threatening! I know the cross will be my tomb.

There's where my ancestors rest—father, grandfather, great-grandfather, and great-great-grandfather."[3]

In their religious environment, Jewish people considered crucifixion *anathema*, and it was absurd to believe in a crucified Messiah. According to the Mosaic Law, "Anyone who is hung on a pole is under the curse of the Lord" (Deut 21:23). Even if the Book of Deuteronomy refers that passage to the exposition of a corpse executed before, it was applied to the crucifixion in Second Temple Judaism. Therefore, the first reaction of Jews against the confession of faith "Jesus is Lord" was "Jesus is accursed" (see 1 Cor 12:3). After the encounter on the road to Damascus, Paul passed from the curse "Jesus is accursed," or *anáthema*, to the confession of faith "Jesus is the Lord," and understood the passage of Deuteronomy 21:23 in a different way. In fact, Christ became a curse not because he made sin but "for us" (see Gal 3:13) and he became "for us wisdom, righteousness, holiness and redemption" (1 Cor 1:30). Against Jews and Greeks who are looking for miracles and wisdom, Paul preaches Christ crucified, a scandal and foolishness to all human beings (see 1 Cor 1:22–23). The scandal of the cross is the center of Paul's gospel and "the cross alone is our theology."[4]

The contrast between the course of honor and the course of ignominy accomplished by Christ is sharp. It stands out if we think that while Roman emperors were deified after death, Christ Jesus was equal to God and in the form of God from eternity, before he had chosen to accomplish the course of shame. His humanity was not the starting point but his goal, because from the divine condition he made the choice to reach our human condition.

Moreover, it was not just a matter of feelings, as the verse that introduces the *eulogy of Christ* (see Phil 2:5) is usually rendered in modern versions. Instead, it is a question of evaluation—that *fronein* (to evaluate)—by which our system of thought is regulated. Today, we could say it is a matter of one's own mental system that the most important choices for life are made. Therefore, Paul does not exhort the believers to have the sentiments of Jesus, which are also important, but above all his system of discernment and evaluation, peculiar to his mindset. In fact, throughout all the eulogy of Christ in Philippians 2:6–11, attention is not paid to his feelings, which are not mentioned, but to two values: humility and obedience. Christ Jesus evaluated and chose to pass from a divine status to a human condition, without excluding anything of the humanity he encountered and brought upon himself.

In this passage from a divine to a human condition, the starting point of the eulogy of Christ is decisive: "Being in the form of God" (Phil 2:6) is the original condition of Jesus, on which depends the rest of his *curriculum vitae.* This starting point is so poignant that it can be rendered in three different ways: "*Despite* being in the form of God" (concession); "*while* he was in the form of God" (circumstance); and "*because* he was of the form of God" (reason or cause). His assimilation to our humanity was not only a divine concession, but also the reason and the circumstance in which Christ Jesus freely decided to conform himself to our human condition.

We find his divine condition and the dispossession he made of himself at the beginning of Christ's course of dishonor. The first condition comes to the second one because Christ emptied himself, renouncing the jealousy-guarded possession of self he had from eternity. The noun that indicates the starting point for emptiness of the self, operated by Christ, is remarkable. In fact, the noun *harpagmon* (lit., "a thing to be grasped") alludes to the most precious thing one possesses, that which one would never want to get rid of.

It is not by chance that Harpagon is also the name of the central character in *The Miser*, a Molière comedy (1668). Christ Jesus is the opposite example of Harpagon, because Jesus's choice was a radical altruism, to the point of annihilation and total denudation of himself. The spoliation of Christ is of a child who is born naked and is stripped of his dignity during his passion (see Matt 27:28). What does such an amazing choice mean for those who are called to assume a similar system of evaluation following Christ Jesus's example?

HE HUMBLED HIMSELF

Humility is not a value and obedience can become the most dangerous temptation! We are living in a time in which humility and obedience are lacking in many places. Rather than values, they are seen as weaknesses. To tell the truth, neither is a virtue, but they manifest themselves as values when the system of evaluation, chosen by Christ Jesus, takes the center of our life. In fact, Paul makes use of the eulogy of Christ to emphasize that these two values come from conformity or from intimacy with him. Let us see how humility and obedience are intertwined and how they become values (more than virtues) for believers in Christ. While a virtue is considered by its power, a value depends on the relationship between people and their environment.

The sequence of the eulogy for Christ starts from humility and ends with obedience. That sequence is not accidental because it underscores how humility engenders obedience and not the contrary. Humility is the source of obedience! If Christ's humility relates the eulogy of Christ to the previous verses (see Phil 2:3–4), his obedience is connected to what follows (see v. 12). Because Christ Jesus humbled himself, even to death on a cross, believers are called to consider their brethren above themselves in humility (see Phil 2:3). The main road for humility does not lie in our temper, or in our natural aptitude to being humble, but it depends on the relationship with the cross of Christ. According to the word of the cross (see 1 Cor 1:18), God has chosen lowly, despised, and useless things, nullifying the things of the world, so that no one may boast before him (see 1 Cor 1:28–29). Humility does not have a positive meaning, but it becomes a value depending on the relationship with Christ who has divested himself even to death on a cross. The paradox of reversal is also the center of the *Magnificat*, the song of Mary. Because God has overthrown the mighty from their thrones, he has looked upon the humility of his maidservant (see Luke 1:48, 52). In other words, Paul thinks of humility as doing nothing out of rivalry or vainglory, but in considering others as superior to ourselves.

However, this ecclesial value does not arise from ourselves, because we are often faced with an affected humility that is hiding its own anxiety of prevailing over others at any cost. True humility springs and is developed by intimacy with Christ Jesus; otherwise, it has no reason to be maintained. Because no one can fully imitate Christ, humility grows from the relationship with him until the end of our life. As Paul emphasizes elsewhere, Christ's love torments and anguishes us so that those who live do not live for themselves, but for him who died and rose for them (see 2 Cor 5:14). If we live for ourselves and our ego occupies the center of our mental system, there is no humility to be kept. Christ's emptiness is the only reason for the humility of believers.

While Christ's example of humility is unattainable, the example of Epaphroditus, one of Paul's coworkers, is pointed out to the Philippians. Epaphroditus belonged to the Philippian community and brought their economic help to Paul while he was in prison (see Phil 4:18). Following the example of Christ, Epaphroditus endangered his life for the gospel "until death" (see Phil 2:30). It is not by chance that the expression "until death" used in the eulogy of Christ (see Phil 2:8) resounds in "until death" for Epaphroditus. As we can see, the utterance is equal and only occurs in these two phrases for the entire Bible. Christ's humility continues and is visible in Epaphroditus's devotion to the gospel. Thus, the unattainable example of Jesus Christ becomes visible and tangible in those who have already imitated him by risking their lives for him and the gospel.

The obedience of Christ is the consequence of his humility. Thus, believers are called to be always obedient, working for their salvation with fear and trembling (see Phil 2:25–30). While Epaphroditus is chosen as an example of humility, Timothy is indicated as an example of obedience. As a son with his father, Timothy had served with Paul in the work of the gospel or for the evangelization (see Phil 2:22). In fact, the precious coworker founded the Philippian community with Paul (see Acts 16:1–12) and he was well known to them (see Phil 1:1). Once again, the unattainable example of Christ becomes visible in those who had conformed their life to his system of discernment.

As we can observe, Paul speaks of humility and obedience without references. To whom did Christ Jesus humble himself? And for whom did he become obedient until death? The eulogy does not specify the addressees of Christ's humility and obedience, because the two values, epitomized by him, assume a general horizon. Christ's obedience, like his humility, is addressed to the Father, to the earthly parents in his childhood, to human beings, and to the time and the space in which he lived, even to the Mosaic Law under which he was born (see Gal 4:4).

Since true humility is a gift, obedience too comes from listening: "Faith comes from hearing," Paul accurately states in Romans 10:17. On the contrary, obedience turns into a negative value when it is not centered on reciprocal listening, but on an empty and inconsistent authority. When it is rooted in listening, obedience is nourished by mutual trust, faithfulness, and reliability, according to the three principal meanings of the word *pistis* in the Pauline Epistles. Believers find in Christ's humility and obedience an unattainable example to which they should refer for all their life.

We have mentioned the obedience of Christ, according to the Letter to the Hebrews. If from one angle Jesus learned obedience from things he suffered, from another angle he becomes the cause of salvation for those who obey him (see Heb 5:9). Our obedience to Christ is grounded on what he learned during the days of his flesh or in the course of his humanity, rather than "during his earthly life," as in many contemporary versions (cf. NIV, NIB, and NJB). Obedience becomes a very high value in mutual listening, when no one person is thinking of himself as superior to the other, but when everyone is listening to the other and we are obedient only to the Word that became flesh (see John 1:14).

Once again, conformity or the connatural relationship between people is crucial: as we are listening to the other, we become capable of a natural obedience. True obedience does not flow from authority, or from our roles in the Church, but from congeniality between people who are able to acknowledge themselves in other persons. For too many centuries, we have thought of the imitation of Christ and of saints as if springs from authority, while according to Paul we should follow a different stream. Humility and obedience spring in a natural way from the intimacy with constant attendance to Jesus Christ.

CONCLUSION

While he was a governor in the Roman province of Bithynia, Pliny the Younger wrote an important letter to the emperor Trajan (first decades of the second century CE). The emperor was asked how to deal with voluntary cultic associations and, particularly, with Christians. As regards them, Pliny adds,

> They also declared that the sum total of their guilt or error amounted to no more than this: they had met regularly before dawn on a fixed day to chant verses alternately among themselves in honour of Christ as if to a god, and also to bind themselves by oath, not for any criminal purpose, but to abstain from theft, to commit no breach of trust and not deny a deposit when called upon to restore it.[5]

Focused on the humanity of Christ, the so-called *eulogy of Christ* of Philippians 2:6–11 explains why for two thousand years up to now believers antiphonally sing to Christ in the evening between Saturday and Sunday. In fact, the canticle of Philippians 2:6–11 is included in all the first vespers of Sunday in the Liturgy of the Hours. Waiting for the dawn of the day without end, believers confess Jesus Christ as their unique Lord.

The eulogy of Christ might have been composed in various situations of the first Christian communities. Because of the descending and ascending movement referred to in the eulogy, baptism has been thought of as its ideal background. Like Jesus Christ, the catechumen is asked to empty himself, and he is clothed with the white dress of baptism. Baptized by the Holy Spirit, believers have been clothed in Christ (see Gal 3:27).

Moreover, the eucharistic context is equally significant because the eulogy of Christ reminds us of the washing of the disciples' feet, done by Jesus during the Last Supper (see John 13:1–11). Like Jesus, the disciples are asked to wash one another's feet following his incomparable example: "I have set you an example that you should do as I have done for you" (John 13:15).

However, in our opinion, the most appropriate context in which the eulogy of Christ was probably composed regards persecutions suffered by believers for Christ's sake. In fact, from the beginning of the letter, Paul gives thanks to God because the Philippians have been granted not only to believe in Christ, but also to suffer for him (see Phil 1:29). The verb "to confess" (rather than "to profess") used in Philippians 2:11 reminds us of the confession of faith in the persecution of believers. We should keep in mind the difference between *profession* and *confession*. While a profession can also be said by those who are not involved, a confession only occurs when a witness has seen with his own eyes and is willing to risk his life for another person.

Therefore, the eulogy of Christ is a germinal confession of faith because, among other things, only imitation or conformity between people makes it possible for a religious movement to survive in conditions of persecution and captivity. The humanity of Christ is the necessary path for the superexaltation he received from the Father and the name, which is above all other names: Lord Jesus Christ (see Phil 2:8–11). Paradoxically, God gave his own name (*Lord*) to Jesus Christ not before, but in and after his death on a cross. How does the course of dishonor or of the ignominy of Christ Jesus become a model for the apostle? As we shall see in the next chapter, Paul rewrites the canticle for Christ with his life. The inimitable example of Christ supports us when we are forced to face situations of captivity and hardships of any kind.

2

Conformed to His Glorious Body

We remain in the Epistle to the Philippians, the delightful letter of joy and conformity to Christ in tribulations. We now move to the paragraph where Paul rewrites the eulogy of Christ with his life, expressing it with an intense pathos:

> But whatever were gains to me, I now consider loss for the sake of Christ. What is more, I consider everything as a loss because of the surpassing worth of the knowledge of Christ Jesus my Lord, for whose sake I have lost all things and I consider them garbage, that I may gain Christ and be found in him, not having justification of my own that comes from the Law, but that which is through faith in Christ—justification that comes from God on the basis on faith. I want to know him, the power of his resurrection, the communion to his sufferings, by conforming to him in his death, and so, somehow, attaining to the resurrection from the dead. Not that I have already conquered [all this], or have already arrived at the goal, but I press on to take hold of that because I too have been conquered by Christ Jesus.
>
> Brethren, I do not consider myself yet to have taken hold

> of it. But one thing I do: forgetting what is behind and straining toward what is ahead, I press on toward the goal to win the prize of God's heavenly call in Christ Jesus. (Phil 3:7–14)

Let us go back to the Basilica of St. Paul outside the Walls and from the majestic apse, where the apostle is depicted while proclaiming the second part of the eulogy of Christ (see Phil 2:10), we look at the central altar. For centuries, it has been considered the place where Paul's mortal relics have been collected and are venerated. A vertical axis relates the representation of the eulogy of Christ to conformity (Phil 3:10) of Paul to Christ by sharing his death in view of participation in his resurrection from the dead. Why, when, and how is the apostle called to conform himself to the risen Christ?

TO KNOW HIM

Before the paragraph devoted to the passage from Christ's humanity to our conformity to him, Paul has enlisted a series of achievements for a *curriculum vitae* of the highest level (see Phil 3:5–6). He used to be a zealous adherent of the Pharisee movement, the most important and influential school of thought in Second Temple Judaism. According to the Acts of the Apostles, Paul was formed at the feet of Gamaliel the Elder and trained in the Mosaic Law of his ancestors (see Acts 22:3). He had been irreproachable about justice by the Law; among other things, he had zealously persecuted the Church of God (see Phil 3:6). Paul had nothing to reproach himself for or to regret in his conduct in Judaism, and he was more zealous than his peers (see Gal 1:13–14). He was not a ne'er-do-well, nor an unfulfilled or a frustrated man because of his inability to observe the Law. On the contrary, he was an adult man, irreproachable for righteousness based on the Torah.

At a certain moment, his irreproachable *curriculum vitae* came to an unexpected turning point for him and for those who knew him well. All the titles conquered in his course of honor became loss and even garbage in comparison with the knowledge of Jesus Christ, his only Lord. Since this sharp turning point, Paul began to rewrite the eulogy of Christ with his own life. From a high status in the religious movement of Pharisees he decided to conform his life to the death of Jesus Christ in view of participation in his resurrection. Christ's course of dishonor is mirrored in Paul's *curriculum vitae* because he chose to reset his course, to assimilate more and more closely to his Lord.

At the center of this turning point we find the same confession of faith for the name that is above all other names and is exalted in the second part of the eulogy of Christ (see Phil 2:9–11): "Lord, Jesus Christ" (v. 11). Nevertheless, he now adds a possessive pronoun full of meaning: "Jesus Christ *my* Lord" (Phil 3:8). While in the confession shared among believers the emphasis is placed on the title "the Lord," now the focus shifts on the pronoun *mine*, which connects "Jesus Christ" and "the Lord." A personal, unique, and unrepeated relationship is underscored: this kind of relationship cannot be duplicated, nor can it be cloned! Romano Guardini very well explains in *The Lord*, his masterpiece, the deep relationship between discipleship and imitation of Christ:

> To be a follower of Christ does not mean to imitate him, literally, but to express him through the medium of one's own life. A Christian is no unnatural reproduction of Christ....The task of the Christian consists of transposing Christ into the stuff of his own daily existence.[1]

All believers are called to conform themselves to Christ, but each one realizes this process of conformity in a personal and original way. Even if the confession of Christ as Lord unifies believers, it differs when people like the apostle Thomas, Mary Magdalene, and Paul are personally implicated. When the risen One appears for the second time among his disciples, Thomas is asked to put his fingers in the wounds of the Lord. The apostle confesses, "*My* Lord and *my* God!" (John 20:28). After Easter, Mary Magdalene explains her crying to the two angels in white robes:

"They have taken *my* Lord away, and I do not know where they have put him" (John 20:13).

The so-called knowledge of Christ is not an intellectual nor an informative process of understanding, but it existentially involves the subjects of the acknowledgment. The focus is on the knowledge accomplished by the communion with Christ's suffering, until death, in view of the sharing of his resurrection. This kind of knowledge surpasses any intellectual sphere and involves the whole human body: mind, feelings, will, and choices. Because of its fullness, such knowledge only comes to an end at the threshold between our earthly life and eternity, when we will see him face-to-face (1 Cor 13:12).

Meanwhile, we are seeing in a confused way, as in a mirror in which we see imperfectly the face of Christ reflected. The insightful metaphor of the mirror offers a good idea of the progressive knowledge of Christ in the life of believers. Paul uses it twice in his letters: in the eulogy of love—more than a hymn of charity—just mentioned (see 1Cor 12:31—13:13) and when the ministry of the Spirit is highlighted (see 2 Cor 3:1–18): "And all of us with a face uncovered, reflecting as in a mirror the glory of the Lord, we are transformed into the same image, from glory to glory, according to the Spirit of the Lord" (v. 18).

Every morning, we look at ourselves in a mirror and have two principal choices: to look at what does appear at first glance, or to see changes inevitably reflected in comparison to the past. The first choice belongs to the narcissist who tantalizes himself thinking of his apparent beauty. The second choice belongs to those who look beyond the visible and are capable of glimpsing what is invisible to the eye. Now according to Paul, while we apparently see corruptible things, we are fixing ourselves upon the image of Christ carried within us, we are transformed day by day (see 2 Cor 4:17).

Therefore, Christ's humanity is visible in the inner life of believers, but it is reflected outside when a paradoxical contrast occurs between levity and gravity, visible and invisible things. While we are usually worried about diseases and their grievousness, according to Paul gravity belongs to our inner man who is bearing the icon of the risen One in him. What appears serious is slight, while what seems slight takes on more weight. As the fox says to the little prince in the famous novel of Antoine de Saint Exupéry, "It is only in the heart that one can see rightly. What is essential is invisible to the eye" (*The Little Prince*).

CONQUERED BY CHRIST JESUS

At first sight, conformity can be understood as a choice accomplished by believers who decide to assimilate their life to Jesus Christ. For centuries, the imitation of Christ has been understood in this way, until it became excluded from various curricula of formation in the Church. On closer sight, the turning point of Paul's *curriculum vitae* is not determined by his choice, which would have been humanly unthinkable. Rather, the radical shift in his life is highlighted by a precise clarification: "Because I too have been conquered by Christ Jesus" (Phil 3:12, lit. rendered). The verb *to conquer* belongs to the agonistic games. It is specifically used for athletes running toward the goal, investing all their strength to win the prize. Paul has already used the same metaphor when he asked the Corinthians to run as in a stadium to conquer the crown that lasts forever (see 1 Cor 9:25). The believers of Thessalonica are praised and called his hope, joy, and the agonistic crown in view of the second coming of the Lord (see 1 Thess 2:19). The metaphor of the agonistic crown is again used in 2 Timothy, where Paul is waiting for the future crown of righteousness that the Lord, the righteous Judge, will award to him and to all those who have longed for his coming (see 1 Tim 4:8). Peter assures the shepherds of the Church they will receive by the Chief Shepherd the crown of glory that will never fade away (see 1 Pet 5:4).

However, the risen One was the first to run toward the goal to conquer the prize. Paul was not only unexpectedly reached by Christ; he was caught to be conquered, like a lover conquers the heart of his beloved. As represented in some medieval cathedrals, the risen Lord and the believer are like a lion that is pouncing on a ram. According to the language of knowledge, just evoked before knowing, face-to-face, at the end of our existence, we have been known and loved by Christ: "Because I too have been known" (1 Cor 12:12) is the starting point for the true experience of love. The risen One has known Paul and has conquered him with such an intense love, producing a new paradox in his life: "For me, to live is Christ and to die is gain" (Phil 1:21). Paul has not despised life with its beauty and human relationships, but everything is devalued in comparison to the knowledge of Christ, his Lord. Human life is evaluated between loss and gain and, paradoxically, Christ is not only the life (see John 14:6) but is Paul's living breath, leading him to consider all the rest as loss. The more Christ becomes the value "to live" for the apostle, the more the apostle is capable of considering the value "to die" as a gain.

At any rate, we should well understand the relationship between loss and gain alluded to in these paradoxical phrases. The man who is speaking is not a Stoic, nor a Cynic who, facing a life without dignity, hopes for the so-called noble death, or suicide. Using the same language as Paul, Antigone declares at the epilogue of her tragedy, "But if I die before my time, I account that gain. For does not whoever lives among many troubles, as I do, gain by death?"[2] Sadly, some scholars have tried to justify euthanasia for believers in Christ, misunderstanding the Pauline sentences about "to live and to die." According to Paul, however, death is transformed from the last enemy (see 1 Cor 15:54–55) into a gain (see Phil 1:21) not because life ought to no longer be lived, but for the sake of our Lord Jesus Christ. Therefore, if from one angle Paul confesses his intense desire to depart and be with Christ, from the other angle he knows that to remain in the body is more necessary for his brethren (see Phil 1:22–24). The more Christ becomes to live, the more to die is transformed into a gain.

CONFORMITY BETWEEN BODIES

To imitate a human being is to be conformed to him, because a true imitation does not come from the authority of the model, nor from our will to imitate him, but from the connatural relationship between people. As he recognizes (see 2 Cor 11:6), Paul does not speak Greek very well because he is a Jew who speaks a Greek influenced by Semitic language. Nevertheless, he becomes a brilliant apostle when he develops the relationship with his Lord Jesus and believers. In these contingencies, he creates terms that we find only in his letters in all the ancient Greek literature before him. We refer to words characterized by the compounds with the prefix *syn-* (with-). Imitation between people is like an artistic one: it is always creative and never a trivial copy of reality. Rightly, Aristotle considers human imitation as "connatural" to human beings:

> For it is an instinct of human being, from childhood, to engage in mimesis (indeed, this distinguishes them from other animals: man is the most mimetic of all, and it is through mimesis that he develops his earliest understanding); and equally natural that everyone enjoys mimetic objects.[3]

In an analogous way, Paul conceives the sharing of the death and resurrection of Christ as a connatural relationship. Since believers have been connatural with Christ in the assimilation to his death, they will be assimilated to his resurrection (see Rom 6:5). Let us now shift to the second part of Paul's self-praise in view of imitation, where he is developing the topics of conformity to the death of Christ (see Phil 3:10):

> But our citizenship is in the heavens from which we await as savior the Lord Jesus Christ, who will transfigure our humble body, conformed to the body of his glory, by the power he has to subdue to himself all things." (Phil 3:20–21, lit. rendered)

Unlike most modern translations, Paul here no longer uses the verb *conform*, as in Philippians 3:10, but the adjective *conformed* to allude to the transformation of our humble body, which will be transfigured in the encounter with the risen Lord. At first sight, it seems that our body will be transfigured when it will also be transformed, and we are naturally thinking about the event of physical death. Our conformity to the body of his glory has already begun for those who await their savior. This kind of conformity began when we were with-crucified (Rom 6:6), "with-buried" (Rom 6:4), and we became "connatural" (Rom 6:5), through baptism, with the death of Jesus Christ. Therefore, our humble body will not be conformed to the glorious body of Christ when we shall meet him in the afterlife. Rather, this process of conformity has already begun with faith in Christ and the baptism into his death. It continues until the moment when our body will be transfigured in the last encounter with our savior.

As we can see, the title "savior" used for Jesus Christ for the first time in Philippians 3:20 is elsewhere taken up in the New Testament, and particularly, in the Gospel of Luke. In fact, at the beginning of the third Gospel, the angel announced the birth of Christ as Lord and savior to the shepherds (see Luke 2:10–11). The savior announced to the shepherds gives salvation to all human beings as for Zacchaeus, the chief tax collector: "Today salvation has come to this house" (Luke 19:9). Jesus promises salvation until the last moment of his earthly life for the man crucified with him: "In truth I tell you, today you will be with me in paradise" (Luke 23:43). Thus, Paul adds two important words to the faith of the first Christian communities: the possessive pronoun *mine*, for the Lord Jesus Christ, and the attribute *savior* to indicate the power allowed to the risen Lord to subject all things to himself.

Conformity between the glorious body of Christ and our humble body or between his glorified humanity and our fragile humanity belongs to the original design of God who has created us for this and has made us a repository of the Holy Spirit (see 2 Cor 1:22; 5:5). We are reminded of the original plan of God at the end of the great song for the Spirit (see Rom 8:1–30) pointing out that those foreknown by God are also predestined to be conformed to the icon of his Son. Those who are predestined are also called, justified, and glorified in Christ (see Rom 8:29–30). All human beings not only take on the icon of God, like Adam and Eve, but they are chosen to be conformed to Christ, the firstborn among many brethren (see Col 1:15).

Therefore, conformity between the glorified body of our Savior Jesus Christ and our own humble body is without end. His humility and his obedience are shared by those who are still running toward the finish line, to win the prize reserved for those who look forward to the complete transfiguration of themselves. Conquered by Christ, all believers are running, like and with Paul, toward the goal of their earthly race.

CONCLUSION

From the divine condition or form, Jesus Christ chose the human form and suffered the death of slaves and of those who belong to the lowest level of the social classes of his time. Similarly, conquered by the risen One, Paul began to conform his life to Christ, renouncing the respectful cursus of honor in Judaism. As Christ did, Paul had freely chosen the course of dishonor and ignominy. He rewrites the eulogy of Christ by recognizing his Lordship in his life. The Lord Jesus Christ became his Lord, in a personal and unbreakable conformity. He confesses Jesus as his savior because he is convinced that, as Lord, Jesus will transfigure our humble body into his glorious one.

Conformity and congeniality rather than imitation! Sadly, the second word is now compromised, and we refuse to imitate others, forgetting that imitation belongs to human nature. Conformity between Christ and Paul began with the conquest achieved by the risen Lord for the apostle. He has elected and conquered the apostle with his love without reserve, until his death on a cross. Conformed to his Lord, Paul began to know him, modeling his life on Christ Jesus and his way of thinking. This kind of conformity begins when we are "in Christ," through faith and baptism, and ends with the transfiguration of our humble body into his glorious body. All the Christian life starts with being "in Christ" and ends with being "with Christ."

We remember two appropriated consequences about conformity between the glorified humanity of Christ Jesus and our own humble body. They occur at the beginning of a deacon's ordination and after the priest's ordination. On the first occasion, the bishop asks the elect, "Are you resolved to shape your way of life always according to the example of Christ, whose body and blood you will give to the people?" A deep conformity is accomplished between Christ, who became the servant of circumcision for his Jewish people (see Rom 15:8), and the deacon called to follow his inimitable example.

Moreover, while delivering the bread and wine for consecration, the bishop recommends to the newly ordained priest, "Receive from the Holy People of God the gifts to be offered to God. Know what you do, imitate what you celebrate, and conform your life to the mystery of the Lord's cross." Our humble body is conformed to the glorious body of Christ, day by day and when we partake to the eucharistic mystery. A conformity like that occurs even if we do not properly understand it or when we need a lifetime to realize it!

3

The Paschal Mystery in the Life of the Apostle

Conformity between Christ's humanity and our life, sketched out in the Letter to the Philippians, continues with the relationship between the apostle and the paschal mystery. To deal with these topics, we need to dwell on 2 Corinthians, the Pauline manifesto devoted to the ministry or the apostolate. To definitively reconcile himself with the Corinthians (see 2 Cor 6:11), Paul opens his heart in this marvelous letter. We can also think of this Epistle as Paul's "Confessions" or his "speech of the body." When his humanity reaches incomparable peaks, his apostolate is preaching with his body. The gap between his own being and the treasure of the gospel is portrayed at the turning point of the first apology (see 2 Cor 2:14–17) as follows:

> But we have this treasure in clay pots, so that this all-surpassing power is from God and not from us. In all [we are] troubled, but not anguished, worried, but not desperate, persecuted, but not abandoned, struck down, but not killed. We always carry on the necrosis of Jesus in our body, so that the life of Jesus may also be revealed in our body. For we, the living ones, are always handed over to death for Jesus' sake, so that the life of

> Jesus may also be manifested in our mortal flesh, so then death is at work in us, but life is at work in you. (2 Cor 4:7–12)

The insightful metaphor of the treasure and clay pots stands out and contains a lot of issues. What does it mean? Why should God have put an inestimable treasure in a fragile vessel? What is the relationship between the necrosis or the progressive consumption of our body with death and life? We will try to deepen the meaning of these images by which the life of Jesus, the necrosis of Paul, and the life of the Corinthians are involved.

WHO IS CAPABLE?

The first apology of 2 Corinthians begins with a deep inquiry: "Who is capable of these things?" (2 Cor 2:16b). The question arose from charges against Paul due to the so-called letter of tears, which is mentioned in 2 Corinthians 2:4. Unfortunately, this letter has been lost and we can only guess its contents. Paul had been accused of peddling the Word of God or the gospel to promote his own interests (see 2 Cor 2:17). Moreover, his opponents charged him with being untrustworthy because he says "yes, yes" to some people and "no, no" to others (see 2 Cor 1:17). Because he had delayed the visit promised to the Corinthians, preferring to remain in the community of Philippi, he is charged with being wobbly or inconstant. From another angle, he himself acknowledges that to receive information about the reaction of the Corinthians to the lost letter of tears, he suddenly gave up the evangelization of Troas to reach Philippi (see 2 Cor 2:12). Fortunately, Paul met Titus in Philippi, who, returning from Corinth, reassured him about the repentance of the Corinthians and their desire to see him as soon as possible (see 2 Cor 2:13; 7:5–6).

In this context, the inquiry about capability in the ministry is quite understandable, and it can be developed in three principal ways. In a negative way, no one is worthy of the gospel or of the Word of God because a very challenging ministry is required. In a positive way, those called to the apostolate become capable because they are chosen as ministers of the gospel by grace and by the Holy Spirit. And because of the apologetic context, Paul first treats the dignity received as a gift (see 2 Cor 3:1—4:6) and afterward the difference between the treasure of the gospel and his own body (cf. 2 Cor 4:7—5:10). The two demonstrations, eventually, come to an end with the section devoted to the love of Christ (see 2 Cor 5:14) and the apostolic service for reconciliation (see 2 Cor 5:11—7:4).

The issue about the human skill needed for the apostolate is not new. It was already advanced at the time of the most tormented prophetic call in the Old Testament. After an endless argument with the Lord, Moses confesses his own inability to carry on the prophetic mission: "I implore You, my Lord, I have never been eloquent, even since you have spoken to your servant, for I am slow and hesitant of speech....Please send anyone you decide to send!" (Exod 4:10, 13). Called to speak as a prophet in the name of the Lord, Moses acknowledges himself to be a stutterer. It was as if he was asked for a job he could not adequately carry out because he was lacking the necessary tools to accomplish it. It would be like asking an ear, nose, and throat specialist to move from his own department to work in cardiology! Each vocation always encounters an initial inability and not a natural aptitude.

Similarly called for his mission, Gideon objected to the Lord that he came from a family of humble origins: "Forgive me, my lord, but how can I deliver Israel? My clan is the weakest in Manasseh and I am the least important of my father's family" (Judg 6:15). Amos was not a prophet, nor did he belong to a prophetic brotherhood. Instead, he was a herdsman and dresser of sycamore trees before his prophetic call (see Amos 7:14). Jeremiah was too young when he was chosen for a demanding mission to uproot and tear down, to destroy and overthrow, and to build and to plant in his people (see Jer 1:5–10). Isaiah was a man with unclean lips who lived among a people of unclean lips (see Isa 6:1–13). On occasion of the annunciation, Mary objects to the archangel Gabriel that she has not known a man to give birth to the Son of God (see Luke 1:35). After the miraculous catch of fish, Peter begs the Lord to get away from him because he is a sinner (cf. Luke 5:8). Finally, remembering the event on the Damascus road, Paul himself admits he had persecuted the Church of God and does not deserve to be called an apostle (see 1 Cor 15:8–9).

On the other side, we find the presumption of a bramble referred to in the famous apologue of Jotham in the Book of Judges. After the renunciation of fruit plants like the olive, the fig, and the vine, the thorn bush willingly accepts to become king over them and give them a refuge with his shadow (see Judg 9:14–15). The thorn bush is promising a shadow or a protection that it cannot give the other trees. When we consider ourselves to be naturally capable for the apostolate, as for any other divine call, we are like a thorn bush. We become like "the braggart soldier" referred to by Plautus in his homonymous comedy.

Paul therefore begins his apology by recognizing his natural inadequacy for the gospel or for the apostolate, along the lines traced by Moses in his prophetic call. The comparison with Moses's call goes through the first part of the apology, and it concerns the veil placed on the face during the revelation of the Lord on Mount Sinai (see 2 Cor 3:1–18). Grace is the decisive filter that allows us to recognize a natural inadequacy transformed into capacity—a grace that overflows in the face of any human difficulties. Thinking about his call to the apostolate, Paul does not forget to underscore the mighty power of divine grace: "By the grace of God, however, I am what I am and His grace in me has not been useless" (1 Cor 15:10). In this sense, the Augustinian and Lutheran axiom "only grace" (*sola gratia*) is very much appropriated. If grace fails, inadequacy is unmasked, and it is not transformed into a capacity to carry out our vocation. What, then, are the gifts of grace that are useful for ministry?

Before drawing out this topic, it is worthwhile to underscore an unbreakable link between Paul's humanity and his apostolate. Throughout 2 Corinthians Paul does not see himself first as a man, and afterward as an apostle, but his humanity is conforming his apostolate, and vice versa. Consequentially, he is not afraid to open his heart wide to the Corinthians (see 2 Cor 6:11), at the great risk of being again humiliated during his next visit in Achaia (see 2 Cor 12:21). If the apostle is sent by God for a prophetic mission, the apostolate pervades his humanity down to the last fiber of his body.

A TREASURE IN CLAY POTS

The first apology of 2 Corinthians is marked by the so-called formulas of entrustment. These kinds of formulas are composed by the verb *to have* and the object or the content of what one possesses. Thus "we have this conviction [or trust]" (2 Cor 3:4), nourished by the gift of the Holy Spirit, and "we have this hope" (2 Cor 3:12) that allows us to behave frankly. "We have this ministry because of God's mercy" (2 Cor 4:1), and "we have this treasure in clay pots" (2 Cor 4:7). "We have the same spirit of faith" (2 Cor 4:13), which allows us to believe and to speak, and finally "we have a heavenly dwelling, while the earthly one is corruptible" (2 Cor 5:1).

The six formulas of entrustment, just mentioned, refer to the gift of the Holy Spirit, freedom or frankness, God's mercy or election, the treasure of the gospel or the presence of Christ in our body, the spirit of faith in order to speak frankly, and the heavenly dwelling not made by human hands. However, we should not misunderstand the meaning of these formulas of entrustment. In fact, they do not refer to what we have acquired by merit or by our human efforts, but to what is given us by grace. To avoid misleading the reader in a different way, we could translate these formulas of entrustment with a phrase like "we have received from God...."

The pathway of the formulas of entrustment in the first apology is worth underscoring. In fact, the first three formulas refer to what makes human beings capable for the apostolate, although no one of them is adequate. Thus, the confidence in the action of the Spirit, hope and freedom give the apostles the power to exercise the ministry because the same Spirit sustains them (see 2 Cor 3:8). The remaining formulas of entrustment also refer to the gifts by which the apostle can continue in his ministry, despite his human inadequacy. In dealing with obstacles of any kind, we receive the treasure of the gospel, the trust between believing and speaking, and the incorruptible heavenly dwelling. The paschal mystery, therefore, conforms the life of the apostle to the death and resurrection of Christ by these gifts.

The treasure in clay pots is outstanding among the gifts we have received. The metaphor can assume different meanings because the clay pot and the treasure are connected to each other. First, the treasure refers to the knowledge of the glory of God in the face of Christ, previously mentioned (see 2 Cor 4:6). In that case, Paul is developing the same topics recommended to the Philippians on which we focused in the last chapter. He had given up what could be a gain for Christ in order to know him (see Phil 3:8). If for Jesus of Nazareth the kingdom of heaven is like a treasure hidden in a field (see Matt 13:44), according to Paul Jesus Christ himself is the treasure placed by God in the heart of the apostle and believers. From another point of view, the clay pot is the recipient of an inestimable treasure. The container is not of iron, nor of gold and bronze, but of clay. Like human nature, it is fragile and weak. To clarify the meaning of the metaphor, we should relate the clay pot to the human being in its integrity and seen in all its fragility and weakness. For example, the member of the Qumran community confesses to the Lord, "And I, a creature of clay, what am I? Mixed with water, with whom shall I be counted? What is my strength? For I find myself at the boundary of wickedness and with those doomed by lot."[1] And in the philosophical environment of the imperial period, Cicero qualified the human body as the receptacle of the soul: "For the body is as it were a vessel or a sort of shelter for the soul."[2]

The link between the treasure and the human body seen as a clay pot expresses various meanings, and we can define them as follows: value, fragility, function, election, and opacity. First, the contrast between the value of the treasure and that of the clay pot stands out because no one would put a treasure in a poor container. Rather, a treasure should be placed in a coffer or in a safe. But the excess of grace overflows by this contrast: God has freely chosen to put the treasure of the gospel in a vessel of clay and without value.

To the contrast between the inestimable value of the treasure and of its cheap container, we can add the fragility of the clay pot. In fact, the vessel chosen by the Lord is not of iron, nor of bronze, but of clay. A vessel of clay can be broken, or it can suffer cracks at any moment, jeopardizing its safety and that of the treasure.

The instrumental function of the metaphor is equally remarkable. The potter can model the clay on the wheel as he likes, adapting the vessel to the treasure. From this point of view, the episode of Jeremiah in the workshop of the potter is noteworthy (see Jer 18:1–6). God sent the prophet into the workshop of the potter, and Jeremiah saw him managing the clay at the wheel. Depending on his purpose, the potter shapes the clay according to his model. The message of the parable is clear: Israel is like clay in the hand of the Lord, his potter, and can be molded as he likes. All of us are clay in the hands of the potter, and nothing else! This is the first mystery revealed in the Book of Genesis, when God formed the human being from dust and breathed the breath of life in his nostrils (see Gen 2:7). As sinners, Isaiah turns to the Lord praying, "But You, Lord, are our Father. We are the clay, you are the potter, we are all the work of your hand" (Isa 64:8).

Moreover, we should not forget the emphasis placed on the divine election, because God is free to choose the people in whom the treasure of the gospel is placed. Paul himself takes up this meaning of the metaphor to underscore God's design, based on his unquestionable election (see Rom 9:6–29). The Lord is always free to choose the clay for different uses, for special and common use (see Rom 9:21), and a clay pot cannot blame the potter, questioning why he made it like this (see Rom 9:20).

Finally, because the metaphor of the clay vessel is used in the context of God's glory and of light in the face of Christ (see 2 Cor 4:1–6), the contrast between the brightness of the treasure and the opacity of the vessel emerges. While we can immediately see the contents of a glass vessel, a clay pot will hide them. The victory of Gideon against the Midianites exemplifies this last meaning of the Pauline metaphor. To win the battle, Gideon used empty jars with burning torches in them (see Judg 7:16–22). Similarly, the glory of God revealed in Christ is hidden in the opacity of our body.

Therefore, the initial inquiry about who is capable of the apostolic ministry (see 2 Cor 2:16) gets different answers, but the principal one underscores the treasure of the gospel placed in a clay pot of little value, fragile and opaque. Nevertheless, God chooses a jar of clay so that it is not human power that stands out, but the power of his grace.

NECROSIS, DEATH, AND LIFE

The paschal mystery is strongly impressed in the life of the apostle conforming him to the death and resurrection of Jesus Christ. To underscore the interchange between the risen One and the apostle, Paul clearly distinguishes death from necrosis in 2 Corinthians 4:10: "We always carry on the necrosis of Jesus in our body, so that the life of Jesus may also be revealed in our body" (lit. rendered). Unfortunately, the distinction is not preserved in most modern translations. Nevertheless, according to the original Greek text, Paul is not speaking of death but of *nekrōsin* produced by Christ in the life of the apostle. Because the genitive "the necrosis of Jesus" refers to the action of the risen Lord in Paul's body, it ought to be understood as subjective and not objective. Now while death, or *thanatos*, occurs at a precise moment of human life, necrosis is progressive, as it unfortunately occurs for some irreversible diseases. Think about some forms of diabetes or incurable cancer. Similarly, believers and the apostle, in the first place, carry in their bodies a process of necrosis or a continuous transformation by which they partake in the death and resurrection of Christ. This same motif of "daily we die" is used by Stoic philosophers in the first century. Seneca's saying in a letter addressed to Lucilius is well known:

> We die every day. In fact, day after day a part of life is taken away from us and even when we grow up, life decreases.[3]

Paul is sharing the motif of "daily we die" with Stoics, but meanwhile he changes its meaning. If for Stoics, like Seneca, the theme of the daily dying is restricted to the personal condition of an individual, according to Paul it plays a relational function. In question is not each person with himself, but the relationship with the death and resurrection of Christ, to which our life is day by day conformed. Therefore, Paul can speak of Christ as his "to live" (and not just his life), and "to die" as a gain (see Phil 1:21). With the language of mysticism, he comes to sustain that he has been crucified with Christ and he no longer lives, but Christ is living in him (see Gal 2:20). Therefore, if he seems to share the Stoic vision of "daily we die," the original relationship with Christ is underscored. And this relationship counts more than the rest of Paul's life.

The list of adversities or hardships, mentioned in 2 Corinthians 4:7–12, may also be considered borrowed from Stoic literature. Like the wise philosopher, the apostle is troubled but not anguished, worried but not desperate, persecuted but not abandoned, struck but not killed. A series of catalogues of adversities begins with 2 Corinthians 4:8–9, and it runs throughout the letter (see the catalogue of 2 Cor 6:3–10; 12:10), until we reach the longer list of 2 Corinthians 11:23–29. One of the most famous catalogues of hardship we find in the Letter to the Romans, where not only the apostles but all believers are involved (see Rom 8:31–39). According to this outstanding catalogue, no one and nothing can separate believers from the love of Christ and of God in Christ (see Rom 8:35, 39). At first sight, philosophers like Epictetus (first–second century CE) refer to similar catalogues:

> Show me a man who though sick is happy, though in danger is happy, though dying is happy, though condemned to exile is happy, though in disrepute is happy. Show him! By the gods, I would fain see a Stoic![4]

However, while Stoics and Cynics relate adversities to the character of the wise man to be tempered, Paul is underscoring the vital relationship between Christ, believers, and the apostle. The goal to be reached between Stoics and Paul is quite different. If apathy or indifference in the face of hardships is the ideal of life worth reaching by Stoics, the deep relationship with the risen One and with those evangelized by his gospel in fact emerges for Paul. Neither imperturbability, nor indifference, but "to be in" and "to be with Christ" is the goal of all adversities upheld by the apostle. As he confesses to the Philippians, "I can do all things through him [Christ] who gives me strength" (Phil 4:13).

Now we understand why the catalogue of hardships ends in 2 Corinthians 4:8–9 with the interchange not only between the necrosis caused by the risen One and Paul's life, but also between the apostle and communities where he is at service. From one side, death is working in Paul's body; from the other side, life is operating in the Corinthian community (see 2 Cor 4:12). A vital exchange occurs between death, which continues to work in the life of the apostle, and his life given for those he has regenerated in Christ by the gospel. These two intercourses are not split up, but they are interdependent, although we would like to avoid sorrows and proofs. Nevertheless, without such a process, one's life is not given to others, and we remain alone and without fruit.

Introducing the section on glory in John's Gospel (see John 13:1—19:42), Jesus expresses the same thought as Paul. If the grain of wheat does not fall on the ground and die, it remains alone, but if it dies, it can produce much fruit (see John 12:24). And Jesus loved his own who were in the world until the end (see John 13:1), to the apex of his life given for his friends. If according to Jesus no one has a greater love than the one who gives his life for his friends (see John 15:13), then for Paul Jesus himself not only died for his friends but also for his enemies (see Rom 5:6). Rightly, nothing compares to the gift of Jesus's life for all humankind: he died for all (see 2 Cor 5:14), not just for many or part of human beings. The inimitable example of Christ sustains the relationship between the apostle and his community.

CONCLUSION

The ordination of deacons begins with the same question posed at the beginning of the first apology in 2 Corinthians 2:16. Asking one of the priests present at the ordination, the bishop says, "Do you judge him to be worthy?" The *diakonia* or the service for the gospel always finds the apostle unprepared and incapable of a ministry difficult to manage. The catalogue of adversities does not need self-pity, or an alibi of any kind. Quite the opposite, human inadequacy is transformed into adequacy and dignity by the power of the Holy Spirit.

Alessandro Manzoni has drawn the character of Don Abbondio in his masterpiece *The Betrothed*, evoking the metaphor of a clay pot. Depicting the meeting with the so-called good men in the first chapter of his novel, Manzoni notices that Don Abbondio "was not born with the heart of a lion." The parish priest is compared to "a vessel of fragile earthenware, obliged to journey in company with many vessels of iron." The metaphor of the clay pot, chosen by Paul to describe the apostolate is like the Don Abbondio description, but how different is the result. Recognizing his natural incapacity, the true apostle conforms his life to Christ and his body is modeled to conform to the precious treasure of the gospel.

However, it is worth pointing out that the protagonist of this transformation is not the apostle, but the Holy Spirit. As the power of God, the Spirit is shaping the clay pot to the treasure of the gospel. The paschal mystery realizes the sharing of the death and resurrection of Christ, because the risen One is producing a progressive and daily necrosis in the life of the apostle. Paradoxically, the result of this interchange done by Christ is not death, but the life of Christ in the necrosis of the apostle. The apostle is daily forced to die a little bit for those he evangelizes, without sparing himself.

The apostle is not a pedagogue, nor a simple trainer, much less an itinerant philosopher, but a person capable of creating a vital relationship with those evangelized by his ministry. His vocation is compared to that of a parent with his children (see 1 Cor 4:15; Gal 4:19), and the apostle remains glad to spend himself and his life for his communities (see 2 Cor 12:14–15). With 1 Thessalonians, we can say the true apostle is called not only to transmit the gospel of God, but his very own life, for those who become dear to him (see 1 Thess 2:8).

4

The Paradox of Grace

The heaven and hell of Paul's life can be defined in the episode described in 2 Corinthians 12:1–10. We ought to read it with the words of Albert Schweitzer, the 1953 Nobel Peace Prize winner and one of the greatest scholars of Pauline thought. In his classic *The Mysticism of Paul the Apostle*, he wrote,

> For when all is said and done, Pauline personal religion is in its fundamental character mystical. It can no doubt find expression for its thought in the eschatological and juridical doctrine of salvation, but its own essential life lies in the mystical. Paul is therefore a mystic. And yet he has not the usual mentality of a mystic.[1]

The passage of 2 Corinthians 12:1–10 concerns a fascinating moment of Paul's life. Meanwhile it is one of the most intricate and debated texts of his epistles. We will try to grasp its principal contents, which are related to conformity between Paul and the risen One.

> We must boast! It is useless, but I will go on to visions and revelations from the Lord. I know a man in Christ who, fourteen years ago, if I do not know with the body, if I do not know outside the body, God knows, he was caught up to the third heaven. And I know that this man—if with his body,

> if without a body I do not know, God knows—was caught up in paradise and listened to unspeakable words that are not granted to man to tell.
>
> Of this I will boast, but I will not boast of myself except in weakness. Even if I wanted to boast I would not be immoderate, I would indeed say the truth. But I refrain so no one will think more of me than is warranted by what I do or say, or because of the extraordinary nature of these revelations.
>
> Therefore, in order to keep me from becoming conceited, I was given a thorn against my flesh, a messenger of Satan to slap me, so that I would not exalt myself. Three times I begged the Lord to remove it from me. But he said to me: "My grace is sufficient for you, for my power is realized in weakness."
>
> Therefore, I will boast all the more gladly about my weakness, so that Christ's power may rest on me. That is why, for Christ's sake, I delight in weakness, outrages, hardships, persecutions, and anguishes. For when I am weak, then I am strong. (2 Cor 12:1–10)

Sufferings and pains are hidden beneath this amazing page of 2 Corinthians. We refer to the sufferings of a man slandered by one from a community he had founded. However, he can evaluate his trials through the filter of divine grace. He had received several calumnies by the Corinthians: a wobbly character, a preacher unable to speak politically correct Greek, the preference for one community above the others, and his unclear management of money collected for the poor of Jerusalem. Finally, because of the lack of visions and revelations, Paul had been charged with not being a true apostle.

It is always true, a person should not be judged by his successes and victories, but when he is defeated and betrayed by his best friends. The allusion to the famous "thorn against the flesh" (2 Cor 12:7, lit. rendered) is one of the enigmatic themes of the paragraph. To whom or to what does a metaphor so awkward refer to?

IN HEAVEN AND HELL

To describe several penalties in hell and purgatory, Dante Alighieri invented the rule of counterpoint and counterbalance in his *Divine Comedy*. According to that rule, proud people were, for example, obliged to push heavy weights with their chests. Narrating the marked contrast between the rapture in paradise and the dreadful adventure of the thorn sent against his flesh, Paul anticipates that rule. He was caught up to the third heaven, and in a sharp contrast, he begged the Lord three times to be freed from the thorn against his flesh. Moreover, while he forgot the words received during his rapture in paradise, he very well remembers the oracle the risen One revealed to him during the agonizing experience with the messenger sent by Satan. While he had been kidnapped to the third sky or to the last level of paradise, his human dignity was severely damaged by the slap of Satan. Nevertheless, grace occupies the center of the scene. Given by the risen Lord to Paul in trouble, grace is sufficient for him to keep going and not to be defeated in trial.

As we know, Paul does not report many "sayings" of Jesus in his letters. The most famous sayings remembered in his letters are the so-called words of institution that Jesus said to his disciples during the Last Supper (see 1 Cor 11:23–25; and the Synoptic traditions of Mark 14:22–25; Matt 26:26–29; Luke 22:12–20) and the "Abba! Father!" prayer (see Gal 4:6; Rom 8:15; in correspondence with Mark 14:36). We can read an echo of Jesus's parables in 1 Thessalonians 5:2: "The day of the Lord will come like a thief in the night" (cf. parallels in Matt 24:43 and Luke 12:39–40). According to the Acts of the Apostles, while he was going to Damascus, a light from heaven flashed around him and the risen One asked him, "Saul, Saul, why do you persecute me?" (Acts 9:4; 22:7; 26:14). The inquiry engendered an intense dialogue with the Lord, and Paul was obliged to recognize the Lord in the Church.

It seems odd, but the only words of the risen One referred to in Pauline Letters are those about the sufficiency of grace, mentioned in 2 Corinthians 12:9. And grace is linked to the power of Christ to afford the weakness of the apostle. We ought to clarify the meaning of that revelation, but its core is occupied by the power of grace. Grace is not only seen as a form of benevolence and charity, but it produces a deep conformity between Jesus Christ and the apostle. It is not by chance that the principal consequence of the paragraph dedicated to visions and revelations underscores the process of conformity between the Lord and the apostle. Jesus was crucified for his weakness, but he still lives by the power of God. Believers and apostles share Jesus's weakness and their future life with him (see 2 Cor 13:4). Not descending from his cross, Jesus had shown the way to redeem every human weakness, and his weakness had been transformed in power by grace. Romano Guardini wrote one of the most appropriated comments about conformity between the weakness and the power shared by Christ and believers:

> The wickedness is still there, but the new beginning as well. The Christian is a battlefield on which the struggle constantly rages between the "old man," rooted in his rebellious self, and "the new man," born of Christ. We must believe in spite of ourselves that we are reborn and bear Christ within us and with him potential glory.[2]

The contrast between the rapture to the third sky and the triple request to be freed from the thorn against the flesh and from the messenger of Satan, is clear-cut. The higher a human being is raised on high, the more he is pulled down! Otherwise, a monument of self-exaltation is created, which is more dangerous than an outward form of narcissism. There is no ecstasy of grace that is not balanced by a trial of sufferings. As Claudius says in Act 3, Scene 4 of *Hamlet*:

> My words fly up, my thoughts remain below.
> Words without thoughts never to heaven go.

WHAT KIND OF WEAKNESSES?

When we try to apply 2 Corinthians 12:1–10 to our daily life, we can think of any form of weakness and a thorn against the flesh of any kind. Paul is alluding to weaknesses occurring during his service for the gospel and for the sake of Christ. As he has well explained at the end of the paragraph, he is thinking of outrages, hardships, persecutions, and anguishes suffered for Christ (see 2 Cor 12:10).

Wherever Paul itemizes a catalogue of hardships or adversities, he never mentions the natural weaknesses or failures of his own character. Rather, the weaknesses for Christ are referred to in Pauline catalogues of hardship. In our case, the thorn against the flesh and the messenger of Satan are mentioned. They humiliated Paul and slapped him, compromising his human honor and dignity. We should remember that slapping a person was one of the most humiliating actions in the ancient Jewish environment. Jesus himself was humiliated at the beginning of his passion; he was slapped by the servants, not by the leaders of the Sanhedrin (see Mark 14:65). On that occasion, the Jewish leaders refused to touch Jesus so they would not be contaminated by his impurity.

As regards the meaning of "the thorn against the flesh," several hypotheses have been advanced: physical disease such as fever, blindness, and epilepsy; psychological illness like schizophrenia, irascibility, and depression; ethical sickness as any sexual turmoil and temptations. In my commentary on 2 Corinthians,[3] I preferred to think of one or more opponents who humiliated Paul in a public assembly, as on the occasion of his intermediate visit to Corinth (see 2 Cor 2:1–11). Not to add fuel to the fire, Paul suddenly left Corinth and reached Philippi, from where he decided to send the lost "letter of tears." However, the thorn against the flesh remains a conundrum impossible to be sorted out with certainty. The few parallels of the noun *skolops* (thorn) with metaphorical meaning in the Old Testament refer to the enemies of Israel. According to the Book of Numbers, the enemies of Israel are seen as "thorns in your eyes" (see 33:55). The prophet Ezekiel says that the house of Israel shall no longer find "sharp thorns among all its neighbors" (see 28:24). Nevertheless, when we think about the reason why one of his opponents humiliated Paul in a public assembly, we are walking in the mist. Related to the thorn against the flesh is the messenger sent by Satan. Who was the anonymous messenger? And why had he humiliated Paul so wildly?

Perhaps Paul does deliberately hide behind the line, remembering the identity of the thorn against his flesh. We can guess it was an outside messenger sent by Satan. In fact, the original expression mentions "a thorn against (dative of disadvantage) the flesh" and not "a thorn of (genitive of specification) the flesh" as in most modern versions. The Vulgate also wrongly had translated the Greek expression *skôlops tē sarkí* with the Latin *stimulus carnis* (genitive).

A trial like that must have been very difficult to bear because, despite his intense and repeated prayers, Paul was not freed from that thorn. Three times he supplicated the Lord to be freed from the thorn against his flesh. Moreover, the situation must have been somewhat prolonged if it required an insistent prayer to the Lord. It is hard to settle further data about the thorn against the flesh, but it can be applied in this way to all those who are suffering beatings, outrages, needs, and similar anguishes for Christ. Among the weaknesses for Christ's sake pointed out by Paul, let us be reminded of the lack of rhetorical ability, the anxiety or solicitude for all the churches, and the prayer.

1. *Profane in the art of speech.* First, Paul recognizes himself as profane in the art of speech or rhetoric (see 2 Cor 11:6), which was highly esteemed in Corinth, as in all ancient Greek society. Remembering his first evangelization in Corinth, he went in weakness with great fear and trembling because he preached not with wise and persuasive words, but with a demonstration of the power of the Holy Spirit (see 1 Cor 2:3–4). In a cultural background characterized by oral or verbal communication, to be unable to speak with political correctness was considered as one of the most grievous faults. In fact, if we, for example, compare the

Greek of Paul's authorial letters, with that of Luke or of the anonymous author of the Letter to the Hebrews, we can see how hard it was for him to manage the Greek speech. Born in Tarsus, Paul was a Jew who lived in Palestine for most of his training (see Acts 22:3). He knows and speaks Greek, but with Semitic inflections or mixed with the Hebrew and the Aramaic of his time in Palestine.

Yet the contents of his letters are fascinating and unique if compared to any other author of his time. Paul's genius dwells in the contents rather than the style of his letters. How he was capable of evangelizing so many Greek cities, despite having learned few of the instruments of rhetorical training, is one of the most difficult questions to be resolved. Let us think about the great contents of the Letter to the Romans or to 2 Corinthians, considered by many scholars as the most difficult and fascinating letters of his correspondence. In our opinion, the success of his evangelization depends not on his eloquence, but on his relationship with Jesus Christ and his adaptability to several situations of his communities. He never evangelized without putting himself in the shoes of his audience. To the weak he became weak to win the weak! Jew with Jews and Greek with Greeks, Paul becomes all things to all people to save someone (see 1 Cor 9:20–22).

2. *The solicitude for all churches.* The second kind of weakness for ministry, mentioned in 2 Corinthians, is the trouble and solicitude for all the churches founded during his evangelization: "Besides everything else, I face daily the pressure of my concern for all the churches" (2 Cor 11:28). In this regard, the sudden interruption of evangelization of Troas stands out. Paul had planned an appointment with Titus in the city of Troas to receive news about the Corinthians' reactions to "the letters of tears." Unfortunately, for reasons we will ignore, Titus did not

meet him in Troas and Paul had no peace of mind. Even if a door had been opened to continue to evangelize Troas, Paul said goodbye to the brethren of the local community and went on to Macedonia to meet Titus. Luckily, they met at Philippi and Paul received comforting news about the Church of Corinth (see 2 Cor 7:4–16). The Corinthians are regretful because they had not defended Paul against his offender in a public assembly (see 2 Cor 2:10). They now hope to see him as soon as possible.

Regarding his communities, Paul does feel a deep jealousy. He speaks of "a divine jealousy" (see 2 Cor 11:2) that remains a jealousy, and it does not admit intrusions of other evangelizers in his field. How great is the humanity arising from Pauline Letters: of a father who every day spends himself for his children (see 2 Cor 12:14).

3. *The weakness of the prayer.* However, the greatest weakness we feel while we pray is not knowing what we should ask the Lord. On those occasions, the Spirit helps us in our weakness, and he intercedes for us through speechless groans (see Rom 8:26–27). We can notice a deep connection between the unspeakable words heard by Paul, while he was caught up to the third sky (see 2 Cor 12:4), and the wordless groans of the Spirit in our hearts. In any kind of prayer—supplication, petition, adoration, thanksgiving, or contemplation—we see a visible weakness and we become more sensitive in relationship with God. In fact, we feel an acute sense of weakness when we pray, because on these occasions we are tempted to give up praying. The worst temptation occurs when it seems as if God is not listening to us. Then we desist from the struggle and we lack perseverance in our prayer. But precisely in these situations we should believe in the most comforting and unique oracle the risen Lord has given to Paul and to all those called to the service for the gospel: "My grace is

> sufficient for you" (2 Cor 12:9). Grace is sufficient while we pray because the Holy Spirit is the power of the risen Lord realized in weakness.

From the content of 2 Corinthians we have chosen three principal weaknesses and sufferings. However, the wide horizon of the passage allows us to comprehend any kind of weaknesses we experience in our life and during the apostolate for Christ. Like Jacob, we are always in the Jabbok River, wrestling like him with the angel of God. At the end of the struggle, our hip or our intimacy is injured, so we should not exalt ourselves before the Lord (see Gen 32:24–25).

THE POWER OF GRACE IN HUMAN WEAKNESS

The keyword *grace* crosses through the gospel in Paul's Epistles. He is always underscoring not merit, but grace, nor the Mosaic Law but gift, nor merit but gratuitousness. We ought to focus on three principal proprieties of grace in his letters: one direction, paradox, and surplus. While it is true, grace never walks two ways, but always is coming from one direction. Grace is not waiting for a correspondence but is subject to the law of benefit. Similarly, the philosopher Seneca can say in his essay *On Benefits*, "In the case of a benefit, this is a binding rule for the two who are concerned—the one should straightway forget that it was given, the other should never forget that it was received."[4]

As long as possible, Paul sustained his service for the gospel at his own expense to avoid creating in people any idea of reward or of quid pro quo. He always excluded any give-and-take between office and benefit to prevent risking the freedom of the gospel. When he was in trouble, Paul accepted being sustained only by the Philippian community because it had sent him money for free and without interest (see Phil 4:10–17). Nevertheless, this is the exception that proves the rule! Evangelization suffers negative repercussions and risks losing its freedom when it depends on human contracts. The only reward Paul is looking for is to preach the gospel free of charge, not to compromise the truth of the gospel (see 1 Cor 9:16–18).

The one directional value of grace stands out in the last marvelous speech Paul gave to the elders of Ephesus in Miletus (see Acts 20:18–35). The apostle is committing the elders to the Lord and to his word of grace, which has the power to build up and to grant them an inheritance among all those sanctified by God (see Acts 20:32). The "word of grace," mentioned at the end of Paul's discourse to the elders, corresponds to "the gospel of grace" named before in the same speech (see Acts 20:24). And "the gospel of grace" ought to be understood as a subjective genitive because it consists of the gratuitousness entrusted to those who freely have received the gospel and freely give it (see Matt 10:8). In disagreement with those who tend to devalue the historical nature of the Acts, the author here is interpreting the heart of Paul's view of the gospel. In fact, the Paul of Acts declares he has no desire for silver, nor gold, nor anyone's clothes (see Acts 20:33) and recalls his listeners of a saying of Jesus not found elsewhere in the gospel: "It is more blessed to give than to receive" (Acts 20:35). Grace as a gift is the beatitude given to those distancing themselves from avarice, simony, and patronage against the gospel.

Moreover, grace is always a paradox because Jesus Christ is its source and the outstanding example. The whole existence of Christ—from the incarnation to his death and resurrection—Paul conceives under the aegis of grace. To sustain the collection for the poor of Jerusalem, he reminds the Corinthians that Jesus was rich and became poor for them, and they became rich from his poverty (see 2 Cor 8:9). God has been involved in this paradox of incarnation because he made sin his only Son, so that we might become the righteousness of God in Christ (see 2 Cor 5:21). An admirable interchange occurred when the Son of God became man. God sent his Son in the assimilation of sinful flesh and condemned sin in the flesh (see Rom 8:3). We cannot understand a paradox like that from reason. Nevertheless, this paradox is so real that if the Son of God had not been assimilated to sinful flesh, he would not have defeated sin. And we become rich of the Spirit of the Son poured out in our heart. As Martin Luther explains in his *Commentary on the Psalms* while he was an Augustinian friar (1513–15):

> This is the magnificent mystery of divine grace toward sinners: by an admirable exchange, our sins are no longer ours, but of Christ, and the righteousness of Christ is no longer Christ's, but ours.[5]

Sadly, the paradoxical interchange between the weakness and power of Christ is always exposed to misunderstandings and devaluations. As time goes by, grace is transformed into a form of acquired right and of human claim. But when Jesus becomes the unattainable example for grace, then an everlasting amazement takes over.

When the Pauline perspective of grace is well understood, it is always in excess or overabundant and it never reaches a point of balance. The comparison between the grace of Christ and the sin of Adam insightfully shows the overabundance of grace: "But where sin increased, grace increased all the more" (Rom 5:20). We come to the core of the paschal *Exsultet* when we sing on the night of Easter,

> O wonder of your humble care for us!
> O love, O charity beyond all telling,
> to ransom a slave you gave away your Son!
>
> O truly necessary sin of Adam,
> destroyed completely by the Death of Christ!
>
> O happy fault
> that earned so great, so glorious a Redeemer!

Christ's grace is enough because it is always superabundant, even when we are afraid that we do not have enough grace. As excess, grace only transforms weakness into strength and human fragility into power. And it is worthwhile to note Paul never does use the union between weakness and strength as an alibi or as a form of a changeless condition. On the contrary, the weakness of the apostle is transformed into power, because that kind of power is given by grace alone.

We now understand why the agonizing passage of 2 Corinthians 12:1–10 ends with the surplus of grace. Paul and all those sustained by the grace of Christ will boast even more gladly about their weakness, so that the power of the risen One, may "set up a tent" over/upon them. We should always keep in mind the verb used in 2 Corinthians 12:9: *episkēnōo* (lit. "to set up a tent" upon someone or something). John is using a similar verb at the turning point of his marvelous prologue (see John 1:1–18): "And the Word became flesh and set up his tent among us" (John 1:14). The tent in question is "the tent of meeting," namely the presence of God's glory during the exodus of Israel in the desert (see Exod 40:34–35). All of us are in exile, and if the earthly tent we live in is being destroyed, God is building for us an eternal house in heaven, not built by human hands (see 2 Cor 5:1).

Ironically, while his opponents are looking for extraordinary visions and revelations (see 2 Cor 12:1) to accept his apostolate, Paul underscores the overlying excess of Christ's grace. Only grace is capable of transforming weakness into power, revealing the presence of Christ in and upon us.

CONCLUSION

The return of Ulysses to Ithaca, his homeland, is one of the most inspired and stupendous episodes of *The Odyssey*. The episode is narrated in the nineteenth book of Homer's masterpiece. After his absence for too many years, Penelope did not immediately recognize her husband. The first person who identified Ulysses was Euryclea, his old nurse, when she noticed a scar on his thigh, inflicted by a wild boar when he was a boy. At the climax of the meeting, Homer comments,

> This scar the old dame, when she had taken the limb in the flat of her hands, knew by the touch, and she let fall the foot. Into

> the basin, the leg fell, and the brazen vessel rang. Over it tilted, and the water was spilled upon the ground. Then upon her soul came joy and grief in one moment, and both her eyes were filled with tears and the flow of her voice was checked. But she touched the chin of Odysseus, and said: "Verily thou art Odysseus, dear child, and I knew thee not, till I had handled all the body of my lord."[6]

Acknowledgment is one of the most important themes in the process of identification and conformity between people. First, it happens when indelible and unique scars are fixed in the body and life of everyone. In a similar way, we ought to understand the meeting between the risen One and Thomas: "My Lord and My God" (John 20:28) is the confession of the apostle when he was asked to put his finger and his hand in the wounds of the Lord. The resurrection does not obliterate Jesus's humanity, but it bears the indelible signs of acknowledgment of faith. Michelangelo Merisi, better known as Caravaggio, was able to draw this form of acknowledgment with great power in *The Incredulity of Saint Thomas.* This splendid painting is today preserved in the Bildergalerie of Potsdam (Germany): Thomas passes from unbelief to belief by recognizing and putting his finger into the open wound of the Lord. He should not be remembered as a doubting Thomas, but as the apostle of acknowledgment.

As we have stated at the beginning of this chapter, 2 Corinthians is the "speech of the body" of the apostle, and we recognize it not by strength, nor by self-praise, but by the weakness transformed into power by the grace of Christ. Paul remembers he had received forty lashes minus one, and three times he had been beaten with rods for the sake of Christ (see 2 Cor 11:24–25). The wounds healed by grace make the apostolate credible and worthy to be lived. You acknowledge the apostle from scars hidden in his body, like Odysseus's scar identified by Euryclea and Christ's scar recognized by Thomas.

Remember the central moment of a priest's ordination, when the bishop is praying to the Lord as follows: "Now, O Lord, come to the aid of our weakness and give us the coworkers we need to exercise the apostolic priesthood." Anxiety and concern for all churches shows one of the most widespread weaknesses in the service for the gospel, because it cannot fill the ever-increasing pastoral and ecclesial needs. Nevertheless, the Lord comes to the aid of our weakness whenever we are supported by his grace. Evoking the testament of St. Thérèse of Lisieux, the parish priest of Georges Bernanos's novel *The Diary of a Country Priest* utters, "What does it matter, all is grace."

5

Manifestations of the Spirit

The Holy Spirit plays a central and an original role in the letters of St. Paul. It is central because believers are always called to live their relationship with the Spirit of Christ or of God. Meanwhile, to talk of the Spirit, Paul uses different and original metaphors, borrowed from the daily life of his communities. The Spirit is the deposit or pledge given in view of its last purchase. He is the promise made, which needs to be filled; the donation for investment of urban works; the power of God hidden in the mystery of the cross; and the manifestation of God working in the body of Christ. One of the densest passages about the Spirit in Paul's letters concerns charisms, ministries, and activities. It was sent around 53–54 CE to the turbulent and noisy community of Corinth:

> As for the gifts of the Spirit, brethren, I do not want you to be uninformed. You know that when you were gentiles, somehow or other you were being dragged and led astray to mute idols. Therefore, I want you to know that no one who is speaking by the Spirit of God says, "Jesus is cursed," and no one can say "Jesus is Lord," except by the Holy Spirit.
>
> There are different charisms, but the same Spirit.
>
> There are different ministries, but the same Lord.
>
> There are different workings, but the same God in all of them and in everyone.

> Now to each one a manifestation of the Spirit is given for utility. To one there is given through the Spirit a word of wisdom, to another a word of knowledge by means of the same Spirit, to another faithfulness by the same Spirit, to another gifts of healing by that one Spirit, to another miraculous powers, to another prophecy, to another discernment of spirits, to another speaking in different kinds of tongues, and to still another the interpretation of tongues. And all these are the work of one and the same Spirit, and he distributes them to each one, just as he determines. (1 Cor 12:1–11)

The passage about charisms and ministries is caused by one of divisions and quarrels arising among the domestic communities of Corinth. While different parties were appealing to one or to the other apostle (see 1 Cor 1:12), the charism of speaking in tongues (or glossolalia) was the principal gift sought in a public assembly. The religious and social environment of Corinth was encouraging this kind of manifestation. In fact, at the beginning of the section, Paul is alluding to the mystery cults widespread in Corinth and in the Mediterranean world. When most of the Corinthians were Gentiles (more than pagans), they were led astray to mute idols (see 1 Cor 12:2). In fact, the mystery cults for Dionysus, Isis, and Osiris were famous in Corinth, and orgiastic meetings in their honor were practiced. To halt this abuse among the believers of Corinth, Paul dictates one of the densest pages about the Spirit, recognizing in him an undisputed supremacy in the life of the Church.

CHARISMS, MINISTRIES, AND WORKINGS

Before answering how we may handle the charism of speaking in tongues, Paul extends the horizon of the question. He distinguishes three kind of gifts operating in the assembly of believers: charisms, ministries, and workings. At first glance, these three gifts seem equal, but they are different and assume their own functions. Charisms, ministries, and workings are similar because of their divine source, but are different for their assignment to the Holy Spirit, to the Lord (Jesus Christ), and to God.

First, Paul assigns charisms to the activity of the Holy Spirit because they are gifts of his grace. The same grace we spoke of in chapter 4 above is called upon for charisms. In fact, the Holy Spirit gives all charisms, distributing them according to his will. Other subjects are summoned in the discernment of charisms, like those called to be leaders or founders of a new movement and religious congregations. Nevertheless, charisms are referred to the Holy Spirit alone in order to emphasize their unity, diversity, and even their costlessness. At this first level, charisms are not determined by an outside agency, but by the inner action of the Spirit. The parables of Jesus about talents (see Matt 25:14–30) or minas (see Luke 19:12–17) anticipate the pathway of the Pauline view of charisms. Before leaving for a journey, a master entrusted different talents or minas to his servants according to his will. On his return from abroad, he asked servants about their investment of the talents or minas received. Therefore, since the Spirit is the Lord, charisms depend on the freedom of his action (see 2 Cor 3:17).

While charisms refer to the Spirit, ministries relate to Jesus Christ, the Lord. The relationship between the lordship of Jesus, mentioned at the beginning of the passage, and ministries or services is not by chance. If "Jesus is the Lord" (1 Cor 12:3), he is the incomparable example for service in the Church. Because no one can confess Jesus as the Lord without the action of the Spirit, charisms become ministries by following the footsteps of Christ. Community takes over in this transfer from charism to ministry or from the free action of the Spirit to the service offered by Jesus to humankind. Jesus Christ, who made himself a servant of Jewish people (see Rom 15:8–9), conforms all kinds of services in a community because his lordship pervades the service that he has done for all. The symbolic action of Jesus washing the feet of his disciples at the beginning of his passion clarifies the linkage between his lordship and ministries in the Church. After he had finished washing their feet, Jesus asked his disciples if they had understood well the meaning of his action. If the Lord had washed their feet, they should follow his example washing one another's feet (see John 13:14).

How great is the paradox that links the lordship and the service of Christ for humankind! The Lord has become a servant of women and men he met during his ministry, giving an example for his disciples. They should not be conquered by the thought of this world. Instead, they ought to serve one another even when they practice the ministry of command. Jesus had been among his disciples as one who serves, and this rule was given to them while they were debating about who should have been considered the greatest (see Luke 22:24–27).

Therefore, while the Holy Spirit gives charisms to those he wants, with unconditional freedom, an indispensable function is assumed by the community in which charisms become ministries. Though all charisms are not transformed in ministries, nevertheless there is no ministry separated from charism. Charisms and institution are linked in this distinction. Without its charismatic root, any institution risks becoming a scaffolding without soul. And without institution, any charism is subjected to the arbitrary will of people and does not become an enduring service. For too long a time, charisms and ministries or institutions have been seen in opposition to one another. Instead, they demand to be seen for their interdependence, without our being confused by their source. While charisms belong to the power and the freedom of the Spirit, ministries find in the Lord Jesus Christ their inimitable reason and example. The freedom of the Spirit by giving charisms becomes service in and for the Church.

Eventually, workings are traced back to God who is working in all things. The Greek word explains why workings are directly attributed to God, more than to the Spirit or to Jesus Christ the Lord. The creative action of God is here summoned because he is still at work in the Church as when the world was created. In this sense, the Church is always in the making—an unending construction. The creative action of God continues in the making of charisms and ministries. Because of the linkage with workings, all charisms are given not for their beauty, nor for an ornamental function, neither to be contemplated, but to become ministries and workings in the

Church. The beauty of charisms and ministries consists in their workings and not the contrary. It is not that nice charisms become useful, but that because they are useful, charisms become nice! Therefore, while not all charisms become ministries and workings, all workings derive from ministries, and all ministries spring from charisms.

A MANIFESTATION OF THE SPIRIT FOR UTILITY

We have just highlighted that charisms are accomplished when they become ministries and workings. We now turn to the addressees and to the purpose of charisms for the Church. As for the addressees, Paul clearly observes, "Now to each one a manifestation of the Spirit is given for utility" (1 Cor 12:7). Against any form of elitism and preference of persons, all the believers and not just some of them are the addressees of a manifestation of the Spirit. The indefinite adjective "to each one" expresses, at the same time, universality and personal destination of charisms. No one is excluded from a manifestation of the Spirit, but all are beneficiaries of it. Paul will explain the universality of charisms when he returns to charisms and ministries in the Letter to the Romans. The universality of charisms depends on the "measure of trustworthiness." Here, he begs the believers not to think of themselves more highly than they ought. Instead, they should think of themselves wisely and justly, in accordance with the measure of trustworthiness given by the Lord to each one (see Rom 12:3).

It is not by chance that the indefinite adjective "each one" connects 1 Corinthians 12:1–11 to Romans 12:3–18. Because the manifestation of the Spirit is given to each one (see 1 Cor 12:7), God has distributed a measure of trustworthiness to each one (see Rom 12:3). We often translate the Greek expression *metron pisteōs* as "the measure of faith" (see NIB, NJB). It refers not to the cardinal virtue of "faith" (see NIV), but to trustworthiness or reliability given by God to all the people. In fact, you cannot confront the virtue of faith between one and another people, but you can compare the inner measure or the stature of people. The measure of trustworthiness corresponds to "the measure of canon" (2 Cor 12:13) given by God to all human beings. Therefore, all believers should measure their inner discernment to understand charisms, given to them to serve the Lord.

Romans 12:3–8 is indispensable in drawing the purpose of the distributive and indefinite adjective "each one." We all have an inner stature and we should identify it; otherwise, we will risk incurring the two deleterious consequences mentioned in Romans 12:3–8: overestimation or, on the contrary, underestimation. Overestimation occurs when, ignoring the measure of our trustworthiness, we try to prevail over others. Careerism, envy, defamation, and slander are the principal consequences of a personal overestimation. Those affected by this inner illness tend to destroy other people in order to exalt themselves. You recognize persons like that when they do not feel good in any place, and they attribute their uneasiness and discomfort to others.

Underestimation is equally widespread, and it corresponds to the condition of those who do not accept themselves for who or what they are. Defeatism, marginalization, and laziness are expressions of a personal undervaluation. They can be compared to the last servant in the parable about talents and minas. While his master was abroad, the last servant buried his talent in a field (see Matt 25:25) or in a handkerchief (see Luke 19:20) because of his laziness or fear of losing it.

Instead, those nourished by a right measure of self are in between these two categories of persons. They are not affected by projects of megalomania or, on the contrary, by an inner tendency to self-harm. People formed to a just measure of self know very well that no one is set apart from a manifestation of the Holy Spirit. Paul is borrowing from the oracle of Delphi widely spread throughout the popular background of the Mediterranean world: "Know yourself." Moreover, he relates that oracle to the measure of trustworthiness conferred by the Spirit to everyone. Speaking of the "measure of trustworthiness," he reminds the listener of the other inscription written in the temple of Delphi: "Nothing in excess." The two oracles are interweaved because to know ourselves depends on taking care of our inner stature and avoiding excess of any kind.

The tongue can be governed; hubris and God can be only feared if we properly know ourselves and avoid excess of any kind in our daily conduct. As regards their purposes, charisms are given not for aesthetics, nor simply to be contemplated, but to be useful for all. Unfortunately, the Greek noun *symferon* in 1 Corinthians 12:7 is not rightly translated by most modern versions: "the general good" (NJB), "the common good" (NIV), and "some benefit" (NAB). But the most appropriate meaning of the word is "for utility." Each manifestation of the Holy Spirit is not only given for good, nor for benefit, but above all to be useful. We refer to usefulness either for those who receive charisms or for the community where they are working. Sadly, there are situations in which a charism is useful for the community, but not for the person who receives it. But cases like that are symptoms of dysfunction and disease that damage the charism, the first addressees, and their community.

Therefore, all charisms are given for a personal and common utility, and not for a community without persons. The sentence of 1 Corinthians 12:7 is well translated by the Vulgate of St. Jerome: "To each one a manifestation of the Spirit is given for *utility*." All manifestations of the Spirit are not only assigned for general or common good, nor for beauty, but to be useful for those who receive them and their community.

ICON OF THE TRINITY

Although Paul does not use the word *Trinity* in his letters, he often adopts some original, implicit, and dense trinitarian formulas. We find one of these formulas in 1 Corinthians 12:4–6, and it is one of the clearest and most beautiful trinitarian sentences. It starts by mentioning the Spirit, gets to the Lord (Jesus), and ends with God. Elsewhere, as at the end of 2 Corinthians, Paul proceeds from the grace of the Lord Jesus Christ to the love of God and the communion with the Holy Spirit (see 2 Cor 13:13). The trinitarian action can also begin with God who has sent his Son and the Spirit of his Son who is crying in our heart, "Abba! Father!" (Gal 4:6; Rom 8:15). The cry of Jesus to his Father during his passion (see Mark

14:36) becomes the cry of his Spirit in the heart of believers. All these variations between the Three Persons are not accidental, but they depend on the level of the trinitarian involvement in human situations. In fact, Paul does not care about the immanent and ethereal Trinity, but his focus is on what the Father, Jesus Christ (the Son), and the Holy Spirit are doing in the life of the Church and of all believers in Christ. In fact, "Lord" is the name of God given to Jesus Christ after his resurrection (see Phil 2:11) and Lord is the Spirit (see 2 Cor 3:17). Their lordship in the life of believers precedes the confession of faith in their divinity.

Entirely turned toward Christian community and to believers, the Trinity is still working in the world and the Church. We see their presence by what the Three Persons are doing in our life and by charisms, ministries, and workings. If we do not read the noun *Trinity* in the New Testament, it is because the early Church lived the trinitarian presence before confessing her faith in the Trinity. Contrary to those who think of the Trinity as a product of gnostic influence or of the history of religions on the early Church, the Trinity is visible when charisms, ministries, and workings are already active in the Church. The insightful and lapidary formula about the Trinity in 1 Corinthians 12:4–6 tells us why and where we ought to confess his presence and action.

First, unity in diversity stands out when the Church is the icon of the trinitarian action. Charisms, ministries, and workings guide us to the original unity of the Spirit, Jesus Christ and God, and Paul always emphasizes unity in diversity. As we know, he is particularly fond of the number *one* often mentioned in his letters. Because all believers are *one* in Christ, there is neither Jew nor Gentile, neither slave nor free, nor is there male and female (see Gal 3:28). Moreover, if by the trespass of the *one* man (Jesus Christ), death reigned in the world, then by the *one* man, we receive grace and justification (see Rom 5:17). Therefore, diversity and variety flow from the unity of the Trinity, and not the contrary. Generated by the Holy Spirit, unity always produces a variety of charisms, without falling into forms of division or, on the contrary, in expressions of uniformity. The process that starts from unity and develops into diversity shows us how the Church is quite different from the republic and from ancient and modern political associations.

The Church becomes an icon of the Trinity not by an acquired idea, but when charisms, ministries, and workings find space within our communities. Otherwise, we will continue to talk about the Trinity in abstraction or according to some theoretical procession. At first glance, the formula about the so-called processions of the Trinity sounds beautiful and perfect, but it does not say anything to the people of our time. On the contrary, we acknowledge or ignore the Trinity from the space we give to charisms, ministries, and workings in our communities. The absence of the Trinity occurs when we only consider institutions without charisms and ministries without workings.

A further visible trace of the Trinity in the making is the heart of the apostle. Using an admirable metaphor, Paul conceives the Corinthians as his letter of recommendation, written on his heart and well known by all people. The Corinthians in person are the metaphorical letter of Christ, written not with ink, but with the Spirit of the living God (see 2 Cor 3:2–3). Jesus Christ is seen as the sender who dictated and subscribed the most original letter of recommendation ever written. The Spirit of the living God is compared to indelible ink with which the ideal letter has been written. God is the One who is giving the Holy Spirit in abundance and without end. Paul is at the same time the secretary, or amanuensis, and the addressee of the letter written in his heart. How astonishing is the metaphor used in 2 Corinthians 3:2–3: the heart of the apostle is the womb of the infinite Trinity!

The agency of the Trinity is not a dream, nor a mirage, neither is it an aseptic dogmatic truth. It belongs to the heart of the apostle and the community in which he is at service. As we can see, the trinitarian action dominates the scene in 2 Corinthians 3:2–3 because Paul is thinking of himself not as the author, nor as the sender of a symbolic letter for recommendation. All his attention is focused on Jesus Christ, and on the Spirit of the living God. Moreover, the heart of the apostle is referred to not because of an intimate or sentimental vision of the trinitarian action, but on the contrary because the Corinthians are compared to a public letter known by everyone.

Therefore, the apostle is reconsidering his relationship with the Christian community from the trinitarian perspective, which allows him to widely open his heart to the recipients of his mission (see 2 Cor 6:11). The heart of the apostle can accommodate those who belong to his community because Jesus Christ is working in it with the Spirit of the living God. Giving space to the Persons of the Trinity means to host and to take care of those who welcome the apostolic ministry. If the apostolate is also called "the ministry the Spirit" (see 2 Cor 3:8), it is because it is at the service of the Spirit and of the Trinity. The Spirit precedes and generates the ministry or the service we give to the Trinity in the world.

CONCLUSION

The first exhortation Paul addresses to his communities by his letters is, "Do not quench the Spirit, do not despise the prophetic utterance" (1 Thess 5:19–20). The two requests are intertwined because not quenching the Holy Spirit means not despising prophecy. In a positive manner, it means encouragement to keep the flame of the Spirit burning and take care of prophecy. Rather than an unnamed prophecy of divination, as for mystery cults, the Holy Spirit gives Christian prophecy for the benefit of all believers. Chosen to be at full service of the gospel and the Word of God, the true prophet does not proclaim himself, but the Lord Jesus Christ (see 2 Cor 4:5). In fact, the first recipients of prophecy are the apostles and through them the community to which they belong.

Having a prophetic identity, the apostle is called to ingest the scroll held by the angel, according to one of the most touching visions referred to in the Book of Revelation (see 10:8–10). On that occasion, John of Patmos hears a voice from heaven asking him to take the scroll from the hand of the angel and to eat it. The angel of the scroll stands between the sea and the land to signify the presence of prophecy in the world. Then the prophet takes the scroll and swallows it. At the beginning, the scroll is sweet like honey in his mouth, but in the end, it becomes bitter in the bowels. Against extemporaneous forms of prophecy in the Church, we should always bear in mind that vision of the scroll. It is borrowed from Ezekiel at the beginning of his prophetic mission (see Ezek 2:9—3:3). Nevertheless, while Ezekiel only tasted how the scroll was as sweet as honey in his mouth, John also tastes the bitterness of the Word of God in his bowels.

In this chapter, we have often referred to the linkage between unity and diversity of charisms, ministries, and workings. As we have seen, Paul is particularly fond of the number *one*: from unity to diversity in the Church, and not the contrary. The most inspiring "hymn for unity," dictated in the Letter to the Ephesians, highlights the movement from unity to diversity: "One body and one Spirit, as one is the hope to which you have been called, that of your vocation; one Lord, one faith, one baptism. One God and Father of all who is above all, works through everyone and is present in all" (Eph 4:4–6).

The "one" contains the rest because it is the beginning of the rest! This inspired hymn of Ephesians is marked by the singularity of the unity from which flows the diversity of charisms, ministries, and workings. And the grace of God is given to each one according to the measure of Christ's gift (see Eph 4:7). The so-called measure of the gift, attributed to Christ in the Letter to the Ephesians, is related to the Spirit of the Lord in 1 Corinthians, without difference of any kind, because the same Lordship is shared by the Spirit, Jesus Christ, and the Father. There is no difference between the measure of the gift and the measure of trustworthiness mentioned in Romans 12:3. In fact, both refer to charisms given by Christ and his Spirit to each one in dependence of his inner stature. We close this chapter with the brilliant poem written by Gerard Manley Hopkins in 1877. In that sonnet, Christ's singularity is seen in the variety of nature and in what Hopkins calls "men's faces":

AS KINGFISHERS CATCH FIRE
As kingfishers catch fire, dragonflies draw flame;
As tumbled over rim in roundy wells
Stones ring; like each tucked string tells, each hung bell's

PUT ON CHRIST

Bow swung finds tongue to fling out broad its name;
Each mortal thing does one thing and the same:
Deals out that being indoors each one dwells;
Selves—goes itself; *myself* it speaks and spells,
Crying *Whát I do is me: for that I came.*

I say more: the just man justices;
Keeps gráce: thát keeps all his goings graces;
Acts in God's eye what in God's eye he is—
Chríst—for Christ plays in ten thousand places,
Lovely in limbs, and lovely in eyes not his
To the Father through the features of men's faces.[1]

6

Our Thirst Has Been Quenched with One Spirit

The First Letter to the Corinthians is an admirable epistle in which the Holy Spirit and believers compose the body of Christ. Water is one of the most simple and touching metaphors about the Spirit and the body of Christ. The Spirit is compared to water we drink every day to fill our thirst (see 1 Cor 12:13). The following extract is a milestone in the history and the life of the Church:

> Just as the body, though one, has many members, and all the members form one body, so it is with Christ. For we were all baptized by one Spirit to form one body, whether Jews and Greek, slaves and free, and all of us were quenched with one Spirit.
>
> And indeed, the body is not made up of one member, but many. Now if the foot should say: "Because I am not a hand, I do not belong to the body," it would not for that reason stop being part of the body. And if the ear should say: "Because I am not an eye, I do not belong to the body," it would not for that reason stop being part of the body. If the whole body were an eye, where would the hearing be? If the whole body were

> an ear, where would the sense of smell be? But in fact, God has placed the members of the body in a distinct way, as He wanted them to be. If they were all one part, where would the body be? As it is, there are many members, but only one body. The eye cannot say to the hand: "I do not need you!" And the head cannot say to the feet: "I do not need you!" On the contrary, just as the limbs of the body that seem to be weaker are indispensable and the parts of the body that we think are less honorable we treat with special honor. In addition, the parts that are unpresentable are treated with greater decency, while the decent ones do not need special treatment.
>
> But God has shaped the body, giving greater honor to the parts that lacked it, so that there should be no division in the body, but rather the various members take care of each other. If one part suffers, all the limbs suffer with it; if one part is honored, all the members rejoice with it. Now you are the body of Christ, and each one of you is a part of it. (1 Cor 12:12–27)

Paul is not the first one who wrote about human relationships using the metaphor of the body and its limbs. Long before him, Plato adopted the metaphor of the body to describe the ideal republic. The great dialogue in Plato's *Republic* about the relationship between the body and his members is famous:

> "And the chief cause of this is when the citizens do not utter in unison such words as 'mine' and 'not mine,' and similarly with regard to the word 'alien'?"
>
> "Precisely so."
>
> "That city, then, is best ordered in which the greatest number use the expression 'mine' and 'not mine' of the same things in the same way."
>
> "Much the best."
>
> "And the city whose state is most like that of an individual man. For example, if the finger of one of us is wounded, the

> entire community of bodily connections stretching to the soul for 'integration' with the dominant part is made aware, and all of it feels the pain as a whole, though it is a part that suffers, and that is how we come to say that the man has a pain in his finger. And for any other member of the man the same statement holds, alike for a part that labors in pain or is eased by pleasure."
>
> "The same," he said, "and, to return to your question, the best governed state most nearly resembles such an organism."
>
> "That is the kind of a state, then, I presume, that, when anyone of the citizens suffers aught of good or evil, will be most likely to speak of the part that suffers as its own and will share the pleasure or the pain as a whole."
>
> "Inevitably," he said, "if it is well governed."[1]

Aristotle, the disciple of Plato, applied the same metaphor of the body and members in his *Politics* (see 5, 1302c–1303a). Moreover, the apologue of the body and the limbs is well known in the ancient Greco-Roman world. It is reported by Dionysius of Halicarnassus in *Roman Antiquities* 6, 83, 2 and by Titus Livy in *History of Rome* (2, 32, 7–23). Livy attributes the apologue to the patrician Menenius Agrippas when, addressing himself to the plebeians, he persuaded them to give up their desertion and return to cooperate with the patricians in the Roman republic. Moreover, the orator Dion of Prusa attributes the apologue of the body and limbs to Aesop and speaks about it in the *First Discourse* addressed to the inhabitants of Tarsus, Paul's homeland. The theme is also used by Epictetus in his *Diatribes* 2, 10, 4–5, by Cicero in his *On Duty* 3, 5, 22, and by Seneca in his *On Anger* 2, 31, 7.

However, Paul is the first who, speaking of the Church, compares it to the body of Christ. As usual, he does not take this popular theme in a passive way, but he rewrites it according to a new perspective. He reconsiders it with such originality that it is worth emphasizing the peculiarities with which he views the Church as the body of Jesus Christ and its limbs. Meanwhile, we can observe how the motif of the body and limbs is spread among

Stoics and Cynics, but it is never used to describe the relationship between God and Israel in the Old Testament, nor in Second Temple Judaism. In fact, Israel is the elect people of God, the bride and the propriety of the Lord, but no one has described Israel as the body of God. To compare the relationship between God and his people to his body and the limbs would have been considered blasphemy for Old Testament and Jewish thought. The transcendence of God for Israel prevented it from attributing the metaphor of his body and its members to his relationship with his people.

Therefore, the metaphor of the body and limbs used by Paul to speak of the Christian community demonstrates how deep is the interchange between evangelization and culture. From one angle, we need to evangelize the culture, and from the other angle, we ought to use the language and system of our cultural environment to communicate the gospel.

ONE SPIRIT IN ONE BODY

Compared to the parallels with the Greco-Roman sources, mentioned previously, the first new content about the metaphor of the body and limbs in Pauline Letters concerns the primacy of the Holy Spirit. Some scholars have tried to find something similar in the contemporary literature of the first century CE, but without convincing results. Instead, whenever Paul is dealing with the body and limbs to describe the Christian community, the agency of the Spirit is emphasized. According to him all believers are baptized by one Spirit to form one body and they have been quenched by the same Spirit. The starting point of this action does not depend on one or the other member of the body, like the head or the heart, but comes on the Holy Spirit. His action is so vital that it is compared to water (see 1 Cor 12:13). Just as the human body does not survive without water, incurring dangerous dehydration, the Church cannot live without the Holy Spirit. Therefore, the original verb used in 1 Corinthians 12:13 ought not to be translated with a simple "to drink," as in many versions, but with "we have been quenched." Because the subject implied is God, who has poured out his love into our hearts through the Holy Spirit given to us (see Rom 5:5), the verb "we were quenched" should be considered a "divine passive."

Taking up the metaphor of the body and limbs in the Letter to the Romans (see 12:3–13), Paul returns to emphasize the vital role of the Holy Spirit: "Do not be lazy in doing good, be fervent in the Spirit, serve the Lord" (Rom 12:11). The exhortation of being fervent in the Spirit is like a bridge between the double request against the negative laziness in doing good and positively serving the Lord. When believers are fervent in the Spirit, they are rescued from idleness of any kind and serve the Lord through charisms and ministries received by the same Spirit.

Moreover, the metaphor of the body and the limbs is developed in the Letter to the Ephesians, where the Holy Spirit again occupies the principal role (see Eph 4:1–16). The believers of Ephesus are exhorted to preserve the unity of the Spirit through the bond of peace (see Eph 4:3). They should recognize the Church as a single body nourished first by one Spirit (see Eph 4:4). As we can see, the Pauline sequence in these three paragraphs does not start with the body, but always with the Spirit. Because it is seen as the body of Christ with his limbs, the Church does not precede, but follows the action of the Spirit. According to Paul, there is not a predetermined body with his members and afterward the Holy Spirit, but quite the contrary. Quenching all believers, the Spirit generates the Church as unity of the body and diversity of members.

Speaking against sexual immorality in 1 Corinthians, Paul had already highlighted the primacy of the Spirit with respect to the body and the limbs (see 1 Cor 6:1–20). Believers have been washed, sanctified, and justified in the name of Jesus Christ and with the Spirit of our God (see 1 Cor 6:11). Thus, because their bodies are temples of the Holy Spirit, believers do not belong to themselves but to Christ, and they should honor God with their own bodies (see 1 Cor 6:19–20). Quenched and washed with the Holy Spirit, believers become the temple of the Spirit and the body of Christ. In this perspective, the metaphor of the body and limbs takes on a new horizon not reflected in parallels of the Greco-Roman literature.

EVEN THE WEAKER LIMBS ARE INDISPENSABLE

One of the best versions of the apologue about the body and limbs in the ancient world was written by the Roman historian Titus Livy (first century BCE–first century CE). According to the story told by Titus Livy, the patrician Menenius Agrippa convinces the Roman plebeians gathered on the Aventine to abandon the strike and to cooperate with the patricians for the good of the Republic (see *History of Rome* 2, 32, 9–12). Nevertheless, comparing the Roman republic to a body with its limbs, Menenius Agrippa considers the patricians and not the plebeians as the principal members of the body. Plebeians are useful for the economy and sustenance of the Roman republic, but they remain servants and slaves of the patricians. In fact, the essential parts of the republican body are identified with the patricians and not with the plebeians. On the contrary, Paul claims that the weaker members of the body are indispensable (see 1 Cor 12:22). According to him, God has shaped the body of Christ, conferring greater honor to the limbs that are lacking it (see 1 Cor 12:24).

We think this new perspective is due to the paradoxical way by which God is working through "the word of the cross" (see 1 Cor 1:18) in the world and the Church. Because God has chosen the foolish, the weak, and the lowly things of the world to shame the wise, the strong, and the noble things (see 1 Cor 1:26–28), the paradox of the cross of Christ extends its shadow to the relationship between the body and its limbs. The great paradox of the Church as the body of Christ is outstanding: the weaker limbs are not placed at the edge or in the peripheral part of the body, but they occupy its core. Therefore, the weaker members of the Church cannot be set apart in favor of the strong, or for a selective view of the body of Christ.

Paul's thought is not too far from Jesus's discourse about the Church in the Gospel of Matthew (see 18:1–35). While the disciples were debating on who should be considered the greatest in the kingdom of heaven, Jesus called a little child and placed him among them (see Matt 18:1–2). The Church is the icon of the kingdom of heaven when, as weak limbs, children occupy the center of the discipleship. Therefore, the disciples must become like little children; otherwise, they will never enter the kingdom of heaven (see Matt 18:3). Jesus chose the little child not for his innocence or purity, but because children represent the weak members of the Church.

When we share the supper of the Lord, the Eucharist always reproduces this paradoxical truth, reminding us of the deep difference between the Church and the republic or associations of any kind. On the contrary, when we do not recognize the body of the Lord, we are eating and drinking our own condemnation (see 1 Cor 11:27). A deep interchange exists between the Eucharist as the body of Christ and his body composed of believers, and this interchange depends on the care for the poor and weak in the Church. But when a sort of schism occurs, Paul's protest is passionate, and he asks the believers to eat at home if they are not willingly accepting each other in a public assembly (see 1 Cor 12:33).

We have for centuries forgotten this deep relationship between Eucharist and community as the body of Christ. In fact, we have reduced the question about our dignity to eat the body of Christ to a matter of personal conscience or to some sort of intimism. Paul does not deny the introspective evaluation of the self, but the principal dignity underscored in 1 Corinthians depends on the care for the poor and weak. They do not occupy the margins of the Church, as did the well-demarcated classes of patricians and plebeians in the imperial Roman republic. Instead, the poor and weak occupy the center of the Church, and they become the most necessary part of the Christian body. To take part in the Eucharist in a worthy manner first means to acknowledge the feeble and poor limbs of the Church as the body of Christ.

When we eat the body of Christ, we become the limbs of the Church, his body. Against the grain, no one before Paul saw the weaker members of the Church as more indispensable than the strong limbs. Nevertheless, a choice like that comes not on populism, but on "the word of the cross" (see 1 Cor 1:18), which occupies the center of the Church and its identity. The relationship between the parts of the body of Christ is not caused by efficiency, nor by utilitarianism, but only by the paradox of the cross. As the motto of the Carthusian order proclaims, "The cross stands steady while the world turns."

TO SUFFER AND REJOICE WITH

When Paul is asked to speak of the relationship among Christ, believers, and the Church, he is always creative in content and language. As regards the first relationship, he does not say that as the body, though one, has many limbs, and all the limbs form one body, "so it is with the Church." Rather, all his interest is suddenly shifted to the relationship between the risen One and believers to clarify, "...so it is with Christ" (1 Cor 12:12). According to Paul, the Church is not a ready-made body that believers may enter. Instead, all believers form the body of Christ by the power of the Spirit and their thirst is quenched by him. Once again, conformity is at work because from one angle Christ assimilated himself to our humanity (see Phil 2:7), and from the other angle believers are conformed to his death and resurrection (see Phil 3:10–11).

At first sight, the shift from the Church to Christ, just highlighted, seems insignificant and without value. On the contrary, it implies that the risen One is present and visible not only in one part of his body, but in each limb. We not only recognize the presence of the Lord in the head or leader of the Church, but in every part of his body, first in those who are weak and poor. If God has shaped the body of Christ by giving greater honor to the weaker parts, we should recognize him in all his members.

The First Letter to the Corinthians wonderfully teaches us to look at the Church not from above, nor as a preformed entity but from below and while it is in the making. If we would like to see the Church from above, and from the perfect relationship between Christ, her head, and the Church, his body, we should read the Letters to the Colossians and to the Ephesians. According to Colossians, the risen Lord is the head of his body, the Church (see Col 1:18). And for Ephesians, all believers are called to become in every respect the mature body of Christ, the head of the Church (see Eph 4:15; 5:23–33).

The two patterns, namely, the presence of Christ in his entire body (1 Corinthians and Romans) and his function as the head of the Church, his body (Colossians and Ephesians), should not be seen in contradiction. Instead, the mystery of the Church is conveyed in a different way by these two Pauline perspectives. In fact, according to the first model, the head cannot say to the feet, "I do not need you" (see 1 Cor 12:21), because Christ is working in both by the Holy Spirit. And according to the second pattern, Christ is seen as the head of the Church, his body (see Col 1:18; Eph 5:23). The link between the two patterns is performed by so-called necessity. Because we have never seen a head saying to its feet, "I do not need you," we cannot imagine a body walking without its head, and vice versa.

Therefore, according to Paul if one member of the body is suffering, all the members are in pain; if one member is honored, all the members of the body rejoice (see 1 Cor 12:26). A transfer like that only occurs when the central limbs of the human body are involved, but not for all the parts of the body. For example, if the right hand is suffering, the left hand can help it, because they are, in part, independent of each other. For Paul, however, a deep interchange occurs between all the members of the Church, because Christ is living in each one of them. Even if believers are unaware of it, the relationship between the limbs in the body of Christ is deeper than the connection between the parts of the human body. We would say with Dietrich Bonhoeffer,

> To be in Christ therefore means to be in the Church. But if we are in the Church we are verily and bodily in Christ. Now we perceive the whole wealth of meaning which lies behind the idea of the Body of Christ. Since the ascension, Christ's place on earth has been taken by his Body, the Church. The Church is the real presence of Christ.[2]

At first sight, partaking of the sufferings of others seems more difficult than sharing their joy. In fact, people usually try not to be involved in the trials of others. However, it is more difficult to share honor and joy than sufferings and pain. While partaking in joy and success belong to acknowledgment, to share sorrows is often caused by piety and a mere compassion. It belongs to real friends to share success, honor, and joy, because "[a friend] is as it were a second self."[3]

Without the acknowledgment of the self in a friend, envy overtakes those who cannot stand the success and joy of the other. Ultimately, reciprocity between the members of the body underscores the mutual belonging to one body. We do not see our brethren as antagonists and enemies, but we mirror and recognize ourselves in them. Certainly, we ought to remember no one is necessary in the Church. Nevertheless, no one can survive without the other, because both are limbs of the body of Christ. Pope Francis has recently recalled 1 Corinthians 12:26 in his letter to the people of God to contrast sexual abuses accomplished in the Church against minors:

> "If one member suffers, all suffer together with it" (1 Cor 12:26). These words of Saint Paul forcefully echo in my heart as I acknowledge once more the suffering endured by many minors due to sexual abuse, the abuse of power and the abuse of conscience perpetrated by a significant number of clerics and consecrated persons....The pain of victims and their families is also our pain, and so it is urgent that we once more reaffirm our commitment to ensure the protection of minors and of vulnerable adults.[4]

Sadly, the suffering of the weaker limbs procured by other limbs of the body is one of the dreadful scandals of our world. It not only risks undermining the identity of the Church, but also the essence of the gospel.

THE LOVE OF GOD BY THE HOLY SPIRIT

The Holy Spirit is like water by which our thirst is quenched, and like blood transfused in our hearts to vivify all parts of the body. Paul uses this touching metaphor in his Letter to the Romans. Because God has poured out his love in our hearts through the Holy Spirit, hope does not put us to shame (see Rom 5:5). If water is necessary to hydrate the human body, blood supports its survival. The outpouring of the Spirit is the offering of God's love for us, without which we cannot form the Church as the body of Christ.

The eulogy of love, rather than "the hymn of charity" dictated in 1 Corinthians 12:31b—13:13, is a masterpiece about love. The love of Christ (see 2 Cor 5:14), of God (see Rom 8:39), and of the Holy Spirit (see Rom 5:5) for humankind remains in its background, and they are not mentioned in the eulogy of love. In fact, here, Paul does not deliberately attribute love to God, nor to Jesus, nor to the Holy Spirit. The Persons of the Trinity are for a while placed behind the scene, while the center of it is occupied by love. Using the rhetorical figure of "personification" in 1 Corinthians 13:1–13, Paul considers love as a person in flesh and blood that we cannot live without.

Nevertheless, a footprint of trinitarian love is left toward the end of such a wonderful page: "Now I know in part; then I shall know fully, even as I am fully known" (1 Cor 13:12). The verb phrase "I am known" needs to be properly understood. It is a "divine passive" because it refers to the love of God, of Christ, and of the Holy Spirit, without mentioning them. In fact, we shall fully know love because we are already known by love. To know a person means to love him in both Pauline perspective and in the Old Testament language.

Moreover, the "I" or the ego and the first-person singular play a general role in Paul's eulogy of love. We can replace it with all the other personal pronouns, but the meaning of the eulogy of love does not change. Paul is not only speaking of himself in 1 Corinthians 13, but every human being is involved. It is quite strange that the "I" of the eulogy of love does not say, "If I do not love," as we often could say. But he utters, "If I do not have love, I am nothing" (1 Cor 13:2). Because of its universal horizon, we can transfer the Pauline eulogy of love from the New Testament and insert it in all the ancient and new treatises about love. You can put it in Ovid's *The Art of Love* (second century CE), and in Erich Fromm's *The Art of*

Loving (1956), but the relevance of 1 Corinthians 13 remains for every human being. It can be chosen as manifest of love for believers and nonbelievers, Jews, Christians, and Muslims, religious and agnostic people. You recognize love not by its name, nor by its source, but by what it can do. Love is inconceivable without action, and actions speak louder than words!

In his great commentary on 1 Corinthians, St. Thomas Aquinas has grasped the essential structure of the eulogy of love very well. Distinguishing three parts in the eulogy, Aquinas speaks of love "in regard to its necessity" (1 Cor 13:1–3), "in regard to its usefulness" (1 Cor 13:4–7), and "in regard to its endurance" (1 Cor 13:8–13):

> And because he [Paul] had promised to show them a more excellent way, he shows how charity outranks the others, i.e., the charismatic graces. First, in regard to its necessity, namely, because without charity the other gifts are not enough; secondly, as to their utility, namely, because through charity all evils are avoided and good is performed, at *charity is patient* (1 Cor 13:4); thirdly, as to its permanence, at *charity never falls away* (1 Cor 13:8).[5]

Love is not evaluated as much by feelings, but by necessity, usefulness and endurance. Against an inflated and trivial idea of love, we should fix in our mind the eulogy of love because Paul is raising the ethics of love to a very high standard. Could we mirror ourselves in the eulogy of love and confess that we are patient, kind, and not envious? Who can say that his love does not boast and is not proud? Is it possible to find a person who is not self-seeking, not easily angered? Is there any person who does not consider the evil received or who keeps no record of wrongs? Who always protects, always trusts, and always perseveres? We are always in debt and never in credit with love! Love is the only debt worth considering in our hierarchy of values. According to Paul, we should owe no debt to anyone but to love one another, because whoever loves has fulfilled the Law and its commandments (see Gal 5:14; Rom 13:8).

We are never worthy of love, because it is the mirror of the Trinity!

Love is not a projection of our ego, but it is a gift from above. Love is not "a dunghill" and we are not compared to "a cock that gets on it to crow," as it is for Ernest Hemingway.[6] On the contrary, "Love is a sacrament that should be taken kneeling, and *Domine, non sum dignus* should be on the lips and in the hearts of those who receive it."[7] Love is the mirror of the Trinity, and we are never worthy to receive it!

However, the Pauline eulogy of love is not a misplaced stone, placed at random in the section dedicated to charisms, ministries, and workings (see 1 Cor 12:1—14:40). Rather, it indicates the excellent way in which all charisms should pass and be developed. Attracted by the charisms that we like, we risk forgetting love on which all charisms depend. In the name of the most important charism, which in the Corinthian community was speaking in tongues, we forget love. But even if we have a faith capable of moving mountains, we are nothing without love (see 1 Cor 13:2).

At the end of the eulogy of love, we find a comparison to faith and hope (see 1 Cor 13:13). The so-called cardinal virtues are indispensable for believers, but love is the greatest of them. In fact, the only one capable of crossing the line of death is love, because we shall know perfectly by it (see 1 Cor 13:12). Faith and hope are not useless because, among other things, according to Paul, faith is working through love (see Gal 5:6) and love always hopes (see 1 Cor 13:7). However, love alone remains forever because, poured out in our hearts as a pledge (see 2 Cor 5:5), it tends toward the fulfillment of a purchase.

Paul uses the metaphor of the deposit three times in his letters, namely, in 2 Corinthians 1:22; 5:5; and Ephesians 1:14. It gives a good idea about the relationship between the Holy Spirit and love. First, the pledge is the advance for a purchase to be completed. If the pledge is not fulfilled, you risk losing any kind of purchase. The Spirit is like the deposit God has placed in the heart of believers (see 2 Cor 1:22). God will never fail in his love for us, because all of his promises become "yes" in Christ (see 2 Cor 1:20). Jesus Christ is the yes of God to humankind and the only no God has said is to himself by sending his only Son, and the Spirit as a pledge.

Second, as a deposit the Spirit is not only given to believers, but to all human beings created in the image of God. According to Paul, a heavenly dwelling has been made by God for us (see 2 Cor 5:1), and he has given us the Holy Spirit as a deposit, guaranteeing what is to come (see 2 Cor 5:5). Echoes of human creation reverberate in these Pauline phrases. According to the Book of Genesis God molded the human being from dust, breathed into his nostrils the breath of life, and the man and the woman became living beings (see Gen 2:7). The Spirit is the vital breath for every human being, and no one can survive without him. This universal presence of the Spirit advances the marvelous passage of St. Augustine, at the beginning of his *Confessions*: "You have made us for yourself, and our heart finds no peace until it rests in You" (1, 1, 5). As a pledge of God, the Spirit produces an unending anxiety in our heart until what is mortal will be swallowed up by life (see 2 Cor 5:4).

Finally, the Spirit is given to us as a pledge to realize the design of God drawn up in the solemn blessing of the Letter to the Ephesians (see Eph 1:3–14). Before the creation of the world, God chose us in Christ to be holy and immaculate in love (see Eph 1:4), and the Spirit is the pledge realizing the project of God until the last redemption of those who are the possession of God (see Eph 1:4). Love as holiness is the original design of God revealed in Christ by the power of the Holy Spirit. Introducing his apostolic exhortation about holiness, Pope Frances properly recalls the design of God mentioned in the passage of Ephesians: "My modest goal is to repropose the call to holiness in a practical way for our own time, with all its risks, challenges and opportunities. For the Lord has chosen each one of us 'to be holy and blameless before him in love' (Eph 1:4)" (*Gaudete et exultate* 2).

CONCLUSION

The testament of Paul to the elders of Ephesus, written in the Acts of the Apostles, is the insightful icon that reproduces the relationship between the Spirit, the Church, and pastors (see Acts 20:18–35). The arbor of Miletus is the ideal scene where the last great discourse of Paul was entrusted to the elders, before leaving for Jerusalem. The author of the Acts reports one of the most original and touching statements about the Spirit in the New Testament: "Keep watch over yourselves and all the flock in which the Holy Spirit has made you as overseers to pasture the church of God bought with his own blood" (Acts 20:28).

To simplify the Greek sentence, most of the new versions insert references to the blood of Christ. But, according to the original Greek of the discourse, we ought to think of God who bought the Church with the Spirit or with his own blood. The trajectory is like the passage of Romans 5:5, mentioned previously. The love of God has been poured out into the hearts of believers through the Spirit given to the Church of God. Thereby, the Spirit chooses shepherds to oversee the flock of God. The shepherds mentioned in Paul's discourse to the elders of Ephesus are not the masters of the flock. Rather, they are custodians of the flock that belong only to Christ and to the Spirit of God. To carry on the mission entrusted to them, the shepherds need the constant action of the Holy Spirit.

If we want to understand correctly the liaison among the Spirit, the water, and the blood, mentioned in Romans 5:5 and in Acts 20:28, we ought to remember the last moment of Jesus's life according to the Gospel of John. Soon after his death, one of the soldiers pierced the side of Jesus with a spear "and immediately blood and water flowed" (John 19:34). The explanation of the father of the Church St. John Chrysostom is well known: the water was identified with baptism, and the blood was connected to the Eucharist and the mysteries. Chrysostom's (fourth–fifth century CE) interpretation of John 19:34 according to a sacramental perspective is also well known:

> *There flowed from his side water and blood.* Beloved, do not pass this mystery by without a thought. For I have still another mystical explanation to give. I said that a symbol of baptism and the mysteries in that blood and water. It is from both of these that the Church is sprung *through the bath of regeneration and renewal by the Holy Spirit*, through baptism and the mysteries. But the symbols of baptism and the mysteries come from the side of Christ. It is from His side, therefore, that Christ

> formed His church, just as He formed Eve from the side of Adam. And so Moses too, in his account of the first man, has Adam say: *Bone of my bone and flesh of my flesh*, hinting to us of the Master's side. Just as at that time God took the rib of Adam and formed a woman, so Christ gave us blood and water from His side and formed the Church. Just as then He took the rib from Adam when he was in a deep sleep, so now He gave us blood and water after His death, first the water and then the blood.[8]

Without denying the beauty of John Chrysostom's interpretation, we think the sacramental interpretation of John 19:34 could be sustained after the previous reference to the Holy Spirit. A wonderful hendiadys is used in the Fourth Gospel, according to which one idea or one thing is expressed by two words. In fact, *blood* and *water* are joined to signify the gift of the Holy Spirit, just mentioned above: "When he had received the drink, Jesus said: 'It is finished.' And bowing his head, he handed over the Spirit" (John 19:30, lit. rendered). According to John's Gospel, believers should not wait fifty days after Easter to receive the Holy Spirit (see Acts 2:1–13). Instead, the moment of Jesus's last breath on the cross coincides with the gift of the Spirit for the world.

The Spirit is delivered on the cross because it is necessary like water and blood for our body. An amazing irony is uttered when Jesus dies. While he is crying, "I am thirsty" (see John 19:28), he gives us the Spirit, or the blood and water from his side. The death of Jesus is the accomplishment of the promises made during his earthy life: "Whoever believes in me, as Scripture has said, rivers of living water will flow from his side" (John 7:38).

The development drawn out in the First Letter of John is now understandable. Speaking of the coming of Jesus Christ in the world, John clarifies, "He did not come by water only, but by water and blood. And it is the Spirit who testifies, because the Spirit is the truth. For there are three witnesses: the Spirit, the water, and the blood; and these three are one" (1 John 5:6–8). Improperly, several versions of the passage refer to three independent realities. Yet here John is speaking of only one Spirit with which Jesus came into the world and is given for the life of the world. If the Spirit as the truth can testify to Jesus Christ, it is because he is, at the same time, the blood and the water poured out from his side.

We do not give enough credit to the Spirit in the life of the Church, even if we need him as the water and blood for our own body. Jesus's side is "the womb" from which the Church is generated by the Holy Spirit or by blood and water: "From the broken heart, the Church is born as bride to Christ," explains the anonymous axiom of the Middle Ages. As God created Eve from the side of Adam, the Church is created from the side of Jesus Christ.

Who am I in the Church? It is the question that resonates at the end of our chapter devoted to the Holy Spirit and Church. In our opinion, we find the best answer in *Story of a Soul*, the autobiography of St. Thérèse of Lisieux (1873–97). While she was looking for the meaning of her vocation in the Mystical Body of the Church, she found the solution in chapters 12 and 13 of 1 Corinthians. The little Thérèse of the Child Jesus explains,

> I understood it was love alone that made the Church's members act, that if love ever became extinct, apostles would not preach the Gospel and martyrs would not shed their blood. I understood that love comprised all vocations, that love was everything, that it embraced all times and places....In a word, that it was eternal! Then in the excess of my delirious joy, I cried out: "O Jesus, my love...my vocation, at last I have found it....My vocation is Love!"[9]

Love is not simply one of the charisms, but the way by which all charisms should be identified and transformed in ministries and workings.

Conclusion

Jesus of Nazareth created the group of disciples at the beginning of his public life in Galilee and asked them to follow him (see Mark 1:17). Paul was not among Jesus's followers, nor had Paul ever met him while Jesus was speaking in parables and making miracles. Therefore, he prefers to speak of the relationship between the risen One and believers as conformity or imitation that corresponds to discipleship and vice versa. At first sight, discipleship and conformity seem completely different if not opposite indeed. Following a master in his flesh and bones is quite different from imitating him without seeing him physically. Nevertheless, according to Paul, the Lord is not a man of the past, nor a man who belongs to another world. On the contrary, the risen One is living in Paul and is truly life (see Gal 2:20). The Lord is working in him by the agency of his Holy Spirit.

Discipleship and conformity are different in language, but they share the substance of the relationship between Jesus Christ and believers. To follow him is to believe in him and imitate him. To follow in his footsteps is to put on Christ by conformity. To stay with him through discipleship is to be in him through imitation. To abandon him is to be separated from his love. To stay with him right to the scandal of the cross is to be crucified with him, partaking in his death and resurrection. Two faces of one coin are discipleship and conformity, because they are unified by the power of the Spirit of the Son. Consequentially, the disciples are called to become witnesses of the risen One, and the witnesses need to remain disciples of the Master until the last. As Dietrich Bonhoeffer says,

> The fellowship of the cross to which Jesus is calling his disciples is the gift of justification of death and of the forgiveness of sins. The disciple who followed Jesus in the fellowship of the cross received exactly the same gift as the believer who was baptized after he had heard the teaching of St Paul.[1]

There is one risk in the liaison between discipleship and conformity or imitation. Because imitation conforms to the risen One, or to the "Christ of faith," we could not be related to Jesus of Nazareth. In that case, it seems as if the so-called historical Jesus who was a great itinerant preacher, an excellent storyteller of parables, and a worker of miracles, would have been useless. To overcome this prejudice, sustained among others by Rudolph Bultmann in the twentieth century, we need to translate the passage of 2 Corinthians 5:16 in a more accurate way. Paul is declaring in it, "If according to the flesh we have known Jesus Christ, we do no longer know him in this way." The expression "according to the flesh" should be related to the verb "we have known" and not to "Jesus Christ" as in the Bultmann's interpretation. In fact, Paul is not thinking of the two conditions of Jesus before and after Easter, nor of the earthly Jesus and the Christ of faith. Instead, his thought is focused on the two ways by which we choose to live our relationship with Jesus Christ, the Lord: whether from a merely rational way or by the gaze of faith in him and in his death and resurrection.

The humanity of Jesus remains the pivot for salvation: "The flesh is the very condition on which salvation hinges" (Tertullian, *On the Resurrection of the Flesh* 8, 2). Using the image of dangerous shipwrecks, Pope Francis rightly warns against two forms of contemporary heresies, called neo-Gnosticism and neo-Pelagianism:

> They are two heresies from early Christian times, yet they continue to plague us. In our times too, many Christians, perhaps without realizing it, can be seduced by these deceptive ideas, which reflect an anthropocentric immanentism disguised as Catholic truth. (*Gaudete et exultate* 35)

Devaluation of humanity, a predetermined salvation, and tendency to avoid the paradox of the cross are the principal items of neo-Gnosticism. Against it, Paul announces a salvation through the humanity of Christ and of believers—not a predetermined predestination of God for saved and lost people, but the cross of Christ as the way of salvation for all human beings (see 1 Cor 1:18). Against a double predestination—for saved and lost people—the only predestination Paul announces for all human beings is to be conformed to the image of the Son of God (see Rom 8:29).

A self-made salvation grounded on our own efforts and without relations with other believers are the hallmarks of Neo-Pelagianism. To point a contrast with this kind of salvation, Paul proclaims a salvation centered on grace, which involves all our body and the Church. Grace understood as paradox, one direction, and surplus is the wall against a dangerous form of Neo-Pelagianism. Languages change, but new forms of Gnosticism and Pelagianism are always lurking in the air.

In our opinion, Neo-Gnosticism and Neo-Pelagianism are unified by old and new mystery cults where the flag of syncretism dominates. It is a sort of "leftover" of different religions, since one is perceived as equal to the other. We often think of mystery cults as a religion of the past. On the contrary, they retain a permanent attraction and they try to corrode the essence of the gospel, which is the relationship among Jesus Christ, believers, and the Church. To contrast these new tendencies of mystery cults, human imitation as conformity to Christ plays an indispensable role because it assimilates believers into his death and resurrection, and into the Church nourished by the Holy Spirit.

As we have seen, the process of mimesis, or of conformity between people, usually emerges when the identity of a group or a movement is threatened, at risk of being extinguished. On those occasions, people feel an instinct to follow and imitate those who have spent their lives in the name of someone else. If the Christian martyrs continually renew the Church, it is because they are giving their life for Jesus Christ. They reproduce the inimitable example of Christ who gave himself for all (see 2 Cor 5:14–15).

Because of various prejudices we have highlighted in the previous chapters, the imitation of Christ is a much-underestimated theme when we read the Pauline Letters. Nevertheless, there is no letter in which he is not dealing with the imitation of Christ among believers. Since when his first letter was delivered, the believers of Thessalonica are praised for their imitation. They became imitators of the churches of God in Judea because they share the same suffering of those churches (see 1 Thess 2:14). After centuries, we continue to debate the center of Pauline theology: Is this center occupied by justification by faith without the works of the Law or by the mystical "being in Christ"? We forget how much Paul insists on the conformity between Jesus and believers.

Throughout our route we have focused on Philippians and 1–2 Corinthians, namely, on three of the seven Pauline authorial letters, which also include 1 Thessalonians, Galatians, Romans, and Philemon. Anyway, imitation between Christ and believers is Paul's first and last word and passes throughout all his letters. Imitation is his first word when the Thessalonians are praised because they are following the example of Christ and of Paul, amidst many trials (see 1 Thess 1:6). Imitation as conformity is also his last word, when Timothy is recommended to hand down teachings he has received from Paul to trustworthy people (see 2 Tim 2:2): "Join with me in suffering, like a good soldier of Christ Jesus" (2:3).

Even the shorter Letter of Paul to Philemon alludes to conformity between people. Philemon is asked to welcome the slave Onesimus as he would welcome Paul himself (see Phlm 17). Intimacy and attendance are the double common threads of Paul's insistence on imitation between people in his epistles. Intimacy and attendance are compared to the relationship between parents and their sons.

The beginning of human imitation is not based on the authority of the model, nor on the ethics of the disciple, but on election between people. According to Paul, God has chosen all human beings to be conformed to the icon of his Son (see Rom 8:29). All the election of God is inclusive, and nothing of his election is elusive! No one is shut out from the election of God in Christ. If the starting point of Christian imitation is divine election, its last step is the acknowledgment between archetype and imitator. Jesus Christ is the unattainable archetype, and believers are called to conform their life to his death and resurrection until the last.

To put on Christ is not like changing our clothes! Rather, it is to be clothed with his Spirit, which from the inner human being reaches the outer in an unending process of conformity. This process of imitation only ends in the last encounter with Christ when our humble body, conforming to him by faith, will be transformed to his glorious body (see Phil 3:21). The principal themes of our journey can be summarized with *The Living Flame of Love*, the insightful poem of St. John of the Cross, where Pauline metaphors about the Holy Spirit reverberate with sublime power:

1. O living flame of love
that tenderly wounds my soul
in its deepest center! Since
now you are not oppressive,
now consummate! If it be your will:
tear through the veil of this sweet encounter!

2. O sweet cautery,
O delightful wound!
O gentle hand! O delicate touch
that tastes of eternal life
and pays every debt!
In killing you changed death to life.

3. O lamps of fire!
in whose splendors
the deep caverns of feeling,
once obscure and blind,
now give forth, so rarely, so exquisitely,
both warmth and light to their Beloved.

4. How gently and lovingly
you wake in my heart,
where in secret you dwell alone;
and in your sweet breathing,
filled with good and glory,
how tenderly you swell my heart with love.[2]

Notes

PREFACE

1. Seneca, *Ad Lucilium epistulae morales* 11, 10, trans. Richard M. Gummere, Loeb Classical Library 77 (Cambridge, MA: Harvard University Press; London: Heinemann, 1971), 65.

2. Dietrich Bonhoeffer, *The Cost of Discipleship* (New York: Macmillan, 1963), 255–56.

3. St. Augustine, *The Confessions* 8, 12–29, ed. A. Cook Outler (Peabody, MA: Hendrickson, 2004), 159–60.

CHAPTER ONE

1. *Politics* 1, 1254b, trans. H. Rackham, Loeb Classical Library 264 (Cambridge, MA: Harvard University Press; London: Heinemann, 1977), 23.

2. *In Defence of Rabirius* 5, 16, trans. H. Grose Hodge, Loeb Classical Library 198 (Cambridge, MA: Harvard University Press; London: Heinemann, 1979), 467–68.

3. *The Braggart Warrior* 2, 8, trans. P. Nixon, Loeb Classical Library 163 (Cambridge, MA: Harvard University Press; London: Heinemann, 1980), 163.

4. Martin Luther, Weimarer Ausgabe (WA) 5, 176, 32.

5. *Letters* 10, 96, 7; Pliny, *Letters and Panegyricus*, trans. B. Radice, Loeb Classical Library 59 (Cambridge, MA: Harvard University Press; London: Heinemann, 1975), 289.

CHAPTER TWO

1. Romano Guardini, *The Lord* (London: Longmans, Green, 1956), 452.

2. Sophocles, *Antigone* 461–64, trans. H. Lloyd-Jones, Loeb Classical Library 21 (Cambridge, MA: Harvard University Press; London: Heinemann, 1994), 45.

3. *Poetics* 4, 1448b, 4–8, trans. S. Halliwell, Loeb Classical Library 199 (Cambridge, MA: Harvard University Press; London: Heinemann, 1995), 37.

CHAPTER THREE

1. 1QHa 11, 23–24; F. García Martínez, *The Dead Sea Scrolls Translated: The Qumran Text in English* (Leiden: Brill, 1994), 332–33.

2. *Tuscolan Disputations* 1, 22, 52, trans. J. E. King, Loeb Classical Library 141 (Cambridge, MA: Harvard University Press; London: Heinemann, 1971), 63.

3. *Letters to Lucilius* 3, 24, 30.

4. *Diatribes* 2, 19, 24; trans. W. A. Oldfather, Loeb Classical Library 131 (Cambridge, MA: Harvard University Press; London: Heinemann, 2000), 357–59.

CHAPTER FOUR

1. Albert Schweitzer, *The Mysticism of Paul the Apostle*, trans. W. Montgomery (Baltimore, MD: Johns Hopkins University Press, 1998), 25.

2. Romano Guardini, *The Lord* (London: Longmans, Green, 1956), 452.

3. *Paulist Biblical Commentary*, ed. José Enrique Aguilar Chiu, Richard J. Clifford, Carol J. Dempsey et al. (New York/Mahwah, NJ: Paulist Press, 2018), 1113.

4. Seneca, *On Benefits* 2, 10, 4, trans. J. W. Basore, *Seneca Moral Essays*, Loeb Classical Library 310 (Cambridge, MA: Harvard University Press; London: Heinemann, 1975), III, 67.

5. Martin Luther, *Dictata super Psalterium*, WA 5, 608, 6–7.

6. Homer, *Odyssey* 19, 467–75, trans. A. T. Murray, Loeb Classical Library 105 (Cambridge, MA: Harvard University Press; London: Heinemann, 1980), II, 262–63.

CHAPTER FIVE

1. W. H. Gardner and N. H. MacKenzie, eds., *The Poems of Gerard Manley Hopkins*, 4th ed. (Oxford: Oxford University Press, 1970), 90.

CHAPTER SIX

1. Plato, *Republic* 5, 462c–462e, trans. P. Shorey, Loeb Classical Library 237 (Cambridge, MA: Harvard University Press; London: Heinemann, 1978), 471.

2. Dietrich Bonhoeffer, *The Cost of Discipleship* (New York: Macmillan, 1963), 269.

3. Cicero, *On Friendship* 80.

4. Letter of His Holiness Pope Francis to the People of God, August 20, 2018, http://w2.vatican.va/content/francesco/en/letters/2018/documents/papa-francesco_20180820_lettera-popolo-didio.html.

5. Thomas Aquinas, *Commentary on the Letters of Saint Paul to the Corinthians*, trans. F. R. Larcher, B. Mortensen, and D. Keating (Lander, WY: The Aquinas Institute, 2012), 287.

6. Ernest Hemingway, *The Snows of Kilimanjaro and other Stories* (New York: Scribners, 1970), 8.

7. Oscar Wilde, *De Profundis*, in *The Works of Oscar Wilde*, ed. T. Gaynor (Teddington: Senate, 1997), 781.

8. St. John Chrysostom, *Baptismal Instructions*, trans. P. W. Harkins (London: Longmans, Green, 1963), 62.

9. St. Thérèse of Lisieux, *Story of a Soul: The Autobiography of St. Thérèse of Lisieux*, trans. J. Clarke, 3rd ed. (Washington, DC: Institute of Carmelite Studies, 1996), 194.

CONCLUSION

1. Dietrich Bonhoeffer, *The Cost of Discipleship* (New York: Macmillan, 1963), 258.

2. K. Kavanaugh and O. Rodriguez, trans., *The Collected Works of St. John of the Cross* (Washington, DC: Institute of Carmelite Studies, 1991), 639–40.

Bibliography

Aristotle. *Poetics*. LCL 199. Translated by S. Haliwell. Cambridge, MA: Harvard University Press; London: Heinemann, 1995.

———. *Politics*. Loeb Classical Library (henceforth LCL) 264. Translated by H. Rackham. Cambridge, MA: Harvard University Press; London: Heinemann, 1977.

Augustine of Hippo. *The Confessions*. Edited by A. Cook Outler. Peabody, MA: Hendrickson, 2004.

Bonhoeffer, Dietrich. *The Cost of Discipleship*. New York: Macmillan, 1963.

Cicero. *In Defence of Rabirius*. LCL 198. Translated by H. Grose Hodge. Cambridge, MA: Harvard University Press; London: Heinemann, 1979.

———. *Tusculan Disputations*. LCL 141. Translated by J. E. King. Cambridge, MA: Harvard University Press; London: Heinemann, 1971.

Epictetus. *The Discourses. Epictetus: The Discourses as Reported by Arrian*, LCL 131. Translated by W. A. Oldfather. Cambridge, MA: Harvard University Press; London: Heinemann, 2000.

García Martínez, Florentino. *The Dead Sea Scrolls Translated: The Qumran Text in English*. Leiden: Brill, 1994.

Guardini, Romano. *The Lord*. London: Longmans, 1956.

Hemingway, Ernest. *The Snows of Kilimanjaro and other Stories*. New York: Scribner's, 1970.

Homer. *The Odyssey*. LCL 105. Translated by A. T. Murray. Cambridge, MA: Harvard University Press; London: Heinemann, 1980.

Hopkins, Gerald Manley. *The Poems of Gerard Manley Hopkins.* Edited by W. H. Gardner and N. H. MacKenzie. 4th ed. Oxford: Oxford University Press, 1970.

John Chrysostom. *Baptismal Instructions.* Translated by P. W. Harkins. London: Longman, Green, 1963.

John of the Cross. *The Collected Works.* Translated by K. Kavanaugh and O. Rodriguez. Washington, DC: Institute of Carmelite Studies, 1991.

Pitta, Antonio. "Second Corinthians." In *The Paulist Biblical Commentary.* Edited by J. E. Aguilar Chiu, R. J. Clifford, C. J. Dempsey, et al. New York/Mahwah, NJ: Paulist Press, 2018, 1341–79.

Plato. *The Republic.* LCL 237. Translated by P. Shorey. Cambridge, MA: Harvard University Press; London: Heinemann, 1978.

Plautus. *The Merchant. The Braggart Warrior. The Haunted House. The Persian.* LCL 163. Translated by P. Nixon. Cambridge, MA: Harvard University Press; London: Heinemann, 1980.

Pliny the Younger. *Letters and Panegyricus.* LCL 59. Translated by B. Radice. Cambridge, MA: Harvard University Press; London: Heinemann, 1975.

Schweitzer, Albert. *The Mysticism of Paul the Apostle.* Translated by W. Montgomery. Baltimore, MD: Johns Hopkins University Press, 1998.

Seneca. *Letters to Lucilius.* LCL 77. Translated by R. M. Gummere. Cambridge, MA: Harvard University Press; London: Heinemann, 1979.

———. "On Benefits." In *Seneca Moral Essays* III. LCL 310. Translated by J. W. Basore. Cambridge, MA: Harvard University Press; London: Heinemann, 1975.

Sophocles. *Antigone. The Women of Trachis. Philoctetes. Oedipus at Colonus.* LCL 21. Translated by H. Lloyd-Jones. Cambridge, MA: Harvard University Press; London: Heinemann, 1994.

Thérèse of Lisieux. *Story of a Soul.* Translated by J. Clarke. 3rd ed. Washington, DC: Institute of Carmelite Studies, 1996.

Bibliography

Thomas Aquinas. *Commentary on the Letters of Saint Paul to the Corinthians.* Translated by F. R. Larcher, B. Mortensen, and D. Keating. Lander, WY: The Aquinas Institute, 2012.

Wilde, Oscar. *De Profundis.* In *The Works of Oscar Wilde.* Edited by T. Gaynor. Teddington: Senate, 1997.